# One-Eyed Charley
## The California Whip

'93

To Kay... who will
find a way—
Cheers,
R.A. Ramstedt

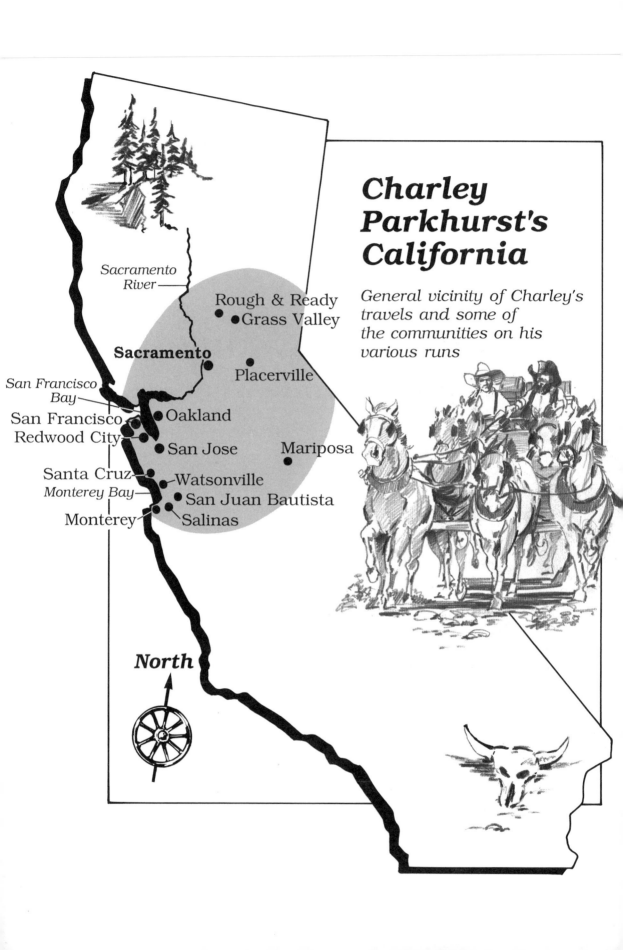

# Charley Parkhurst's California

General vicinity of Charley's travels and some of the communities on his various runs

Sacramento River

Rough & Ready
Grass Valley

Sacramento

Placerville

San Francisco Bay

San Francisco
Redwood City

Oakland

San Jose

Mariposa

Santa Cruz
Monterey Bay

Watsonville

San Juan Bautista

Monterey

Salinas

**North**

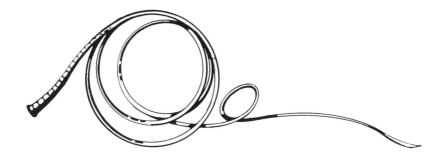

# One-Eyed Charley
## The California Whip

### Randall A. Reinstedt

Illustrated by Ed Greco

*Ghost Town Publications*
*Carmel, California*

Randall A. Reinstedt's
**History & Happenings of California Series**
Ghost Town Publications
P.O. Drawer 5998
Carmel, CA 93921

Manufactured in the United States of America

Library of Congress Catalog Number 90-081382
ISBN 0-933818-23-8


Edited by John Bergez
Book and cover design by John Edeen

*This book is dedicated to Charley,
and to those who find a way*

MARGARET

MR. PERKINS

MISS McCABE

# Knights of the Road

"Peter! Peter Huff, you come back here with that baseball!"

Margaret was yelling at the top of her lungs as she chased Peter around a corner of Manchester School. She was mad! It wasn't just that Peter had spoiled her game of catch by snatching the throw she had made to her younger brother, Alex. What made her positively *red* with fury was what he had *said* as he ran away with the ball.

"*Girls* can't be baseball players, you know!"

And then Alex and the other boys had gone off with him! Oh, how Peter made her furious sometimes!

"Peter!" Margaret yelled again. "Pablo! Jimmy! Come back here! Alex!" Intent on catching the boys, she put her head down to run as fast as she could—and ran smack into a well-dressed gentleman who was making his way up the dirt driveway to the one-room schoolhouse.

"Whoa, slow down!" the man exclaimed as he dropped the satchel he was carrying and grabbed onto Margaret to keep her from falling. "What have we got here, a runaway horse?"

"Sorry," Margaret panted as she recovered her footing. Looking up, she recognized the smiling face of Mr. Perkins, Manchester's new town banker. "Mr. Perkins!" she cried, gulping for breath. "What are you doing here?"

"Gettin' run over, apparently!" Mr. Perkins answered good-naturedly, pushing his glasses back into place.

"Margaret, you really must watch where you're going!" scolded Miss McCabe, the schoolteacher, as she came hurrying down the schoolhouse steps. Stooping to pick up the satchel, she handed it to Mr. Perkins. "Good morning, Harold. Are you quite all right?"

"'Mornin', Miss McCabe," Mr. Perkins smiled, lifting his hat politely. "Yes, I'm just fine. And don't be too hard on the little miss—er, Margaret, is it?"

Margaret nodded. "I'm Margaret Kincaid," she said, breathing more easily now. "'Course, I know who you are, Mr. Perkins. I saw you the other day when my mother went to the bank with the money from the general store."

"Sara Kincaid's daughter, of course! I should have recognized you, but bein' new in town, I don't have everybody straight yet. Well, I'm glad to make your acquaintance, Miss. Your mother's a fine storekeeper, I understand." The banker turned to Miss McCabe. "As I was sayin', Miss Kincaid here had the right of way. She was just in a mighty big hurry, and I didn't see her comin' quite fast enough."

"I *am* sorry," Margaret repeated. "I was so mad I wasn't paying attention."

"And what were you so angry about?" Miss McCabe asked.

"It's that no-good Peter," Margaret said hotly, pointing across the schoolyard, where Peter and the other boys had stopped to toss the ball back and forth. "He and Pablo and the other boys took the baseball and won't let me play—and it's my ball!"

"Dear, dear, is it Boys-versus-Girl again?" Miss McCabe shook her head ruefully. "Peter's our oldest student," she explained to Mr. Perkins. "He's about to turn eleven, and he has little use for girls. Unfortunately for Margaret, with so many families leaving Manchester, she's the only girl left in the school. And the boys all tend to follow Peter's lead, I'm afraid."

"Even Alex!" Margaret added bitterly. "My own brother!"

"The only girl!" Mr. Perkins repeated in surprise. "Is that a fact?" He shook his head. "Well, well. I heard this old one-room school was closin' down after this year, but just one girl! That must get pretty lonesome for you, young lady."

Margaret made a face. "It's not that it's lonesome, Mr. Perkins. It's that it's not *fair.* I'll never get to play any of the games—unless I wake up one morning and find out I've turned into a boy!"

"Oh, you wouldn't want to do that!" Mr. Perkins said with a smile. "You just need to be a little patient with those fellas. In a few years, they'll discover what they've been missin' out on all this time they've been ignorin' you." Shading his eyes against the morning sun, Mr. Perkins looked across the schoolyard. "So these are the young folk I'm speakin' to today, are they? Well, if I'm goin' to be fed to the lions, I may as well know who they are. Let me see if I can figure out who's who. Peter bein' the oldest, he's probably the biggest, too. So I'm guessin' that the husky boy with the big shoulders must be Peter."

"That's right," Margaret said. "Peter's the fifth grade."

"You mean he's *in* the fifth grade," Mr. Perkins corrected her.

"No, he *is* the fifth grade," Miss McCabe laughed. "You see, Peter is our *only* fifth-grader."

"That's his nickname," Margaret added. "We call him Fifth Grade Huff." With a giggle, she added, "He's *big* enough to be the fifth grade!"

Mr. Perkins chuckled. "I see. Now, I think you mentioned a Pablo. I'm bettin' he's that slender boy standing next to Peter."

"Uh-huh. Pablo and I are the fourth grade. He's real smart. And Jimmy Lee and Alex are the third grade."

"Jimmy Lee, eh? I suppose that's the little Chinese boy, since all that's left is the red-haired fella, and he must be brother Alex."

"*Traitor* Alex," sniffed Margaret, watching her little brother taking a toss from Peter.

"Now, now, Margaret," Miss McCabe said soothingly. "I realize it's been difficult for you here, but things will be different next year. You'll be in a big school with real grades, and more children your own age—boys *and* girls—to be friends with. In the meantime, I'll speak with Peter again about—oh-oh, watch out, Harold!"

Spinning around, Mr. Perkins saw the baseball flying straight for his hat and ducked just in time. With a jump Margaret reached high and slapped the ball down.

"Ow!" she cried, waving her hand. "That stings!"

"Hey, thanks, Sis!" called Alex as he came rushing up after the ball.

"Alex!" Miss McCabe said sternly.

"Oh, uh, sorry, Miss McCabe," Alex said sheepishly. "And you, too, Mister. See, Pablo wanted to throw me a long one, and he threw it a little *too* long."

"Well, well, I must say bein' a guest speaker can be hazardous to your health!" Mr. Perkins remarked as he took off his hat and knocked it back into shape where he had grabbed it.

"Only at recess time," Miss McCabe sighed.

"Hey, Alex, throw the ball!" yelled Pablo from across the schoolyard.

"Hurry up, Alex!" Peter shouted. "It's almost time to go back in!"

"*I'll* throw it, Alex," Margaret said decisively as she stooped down and picked up the baseball. "Excuse me, Mr. Perkins." She cupped her hand to her mouth. "This one's for you, Peter!" she yelled. Taking a few running steps, Margaret reared back and let loose a long, high throw that sent the ball sailing across the schoolyard. The boys turned to watch as the ball cleared a low line of trees and disappeared into the long brown grass on the other side.

"What's the matter, Peter? Can't catch?" Margaret shouted.

"Aw, Sis, why did you have to go and do that?" Alex complained. "Now we'll have to go hunting for it at lunchtime."

"*That*," Margaret huffed, "serves you right."

"Dear, dear," said Miss McCabe. "Perhaps we should take shelter inside and get settled for your talk, Harold."

"Suits me fine," Mr. Perkins replied. "This schoolyard is no place for an old codger like me."

"Come along with us, Margaret," Miss McCabe directed. "You can fetch a pitcher of water in case Mr. Perkins starts to feel a little dry in this hot weather."

"What are you going to talk about, Mr. Perkins?" Margaret asked curiously as they climbed the steps of the one-room schoolhouse. "Are you going to teach us about banking?"

"Why, no," Mr. Perkins replied. "Hasn't Miss McCabe explained about my comin' today?"

"I've kept it a surprise," Miss McCabe smiled. "In fact, all the grades are expecting arithmetic tests today. They should be *very* attentive, Harold, when they consider the alternative!"

Mr. Perkins winked at Margaret. "Now *there's* a smart teacher for you. My goodness, what in blazes is that?" The banker gave a little jump as an ear-shattering noise split the air.

Margaret giggled. "That's just the buzzer," she shouted. "It means it's time to go back inside."

"A bit of foolishness, if you ask me," Miss McCabe commented after the buzzer had stopped. "Ever since people started drifting away from Manchester before the Great War, anybody could see that the school would have to close one day. But when they put up the electricity lines in town last year, the school board voted to have this modern buzzer put in. I don't know what they were thinking of. This may be 1920, but a simple old-fashioned bell would do nicely, thank you!"

"That's progress for you," Mr. Perkins grumbled to Margaret. "In my day, the school bell was a hand-held thing that sat on the teacher's desk." With a shudder, he glanced up at the buzzer. "Back then, nobody thought it was necessary to wake up the dead just to tell 'em recess was over."

Miss McCabe tapped her foot impatiently as Manchester School's tiny group of students filed into the one-room schoolhouse and settled into their wooden seats. The boys looked curiously at Mr. Perkins as he set his satchel down on the floor by the big teacher's desk and stood patiently to one side, waiting to be introduced. Margaret arranged a pitcher of water and a glass on Miss McCabe's desk and took her place at her own desk, which was right in front of Peter's.

As she slipped into her seat, Margaret could hear Peter whispering something about "the old guy" to Pablo, who sat across the aisle from her. She was about to turn around and say Mr. Perkins wasn't *that* old when Miss McCabe rapped her wooden pointer on her desk.

"If we're all *quite* back from recess . . ." the teacher began, looking sternly at Peter. Margaret stifled a smile, and she could see that Mr. Perkins was doing the same.

"We have an unusual treat today," Miss McCabe went on. "Many of you probably haven't yet met our guest, Mr.

Perkins, who has just moved to Manchester to run our little bank. He has graciously come to talk to us about a fascinating period in California history, the mining days here in the Sierras. If I'm not mistaken, he will tell us especially about some real heroes of those times—the drivers who drove the stagecoaches through the Gold Country. You see, besides being a banker, Mr. Perkins is a former newspaperman, and quite an expert on the history of the area, I understand."

"Oh hardly that, ma'am," said Mr. Perkins modestly. "Learnin' about the old days is something of a hobby of mine, that's all."

"Nevertheless," Miss McCabe insisted politely, "I'm sure you will find that Mr. Perkins is quite knowledgeable about his subject. Now please listen courteously, and pay attention." With a sly smile, she added, "There just *might* be a test about what we learn today." As the boys groaned, Miss McCabe moved to the side of the room and nodded to Mr. Perkins to begin.

Mr. Perkins looked about the room, and for a moment it seemed to Margaret as if he didn't know quite how to start. She smiled encouragingly at him, and she saw him give a little smile back.

"Well—hrrmph—good morning, boys and girls," the banker said at last. "Er, I guess I mean boys and *girl*," he corrected himself, nodding to Margaret. "I must say I'm findin' it a bit strange to be up here talkin' in front of you. I've done a number of things in my time—some farmin', and some railroadin', and some newspaperin', among others—but bein' a schoolmarm surely isn't one of 'em!" Mr. Perkins grinned. "'Course, lately bankin's been more my line, which is why I was asked to come up here to Manchester when old Mrs. Clampett passed away. They didn't tell me then that the job included runnin' the town post office too! I'll tell you, that Mrs. Clampett must have been quite a woman, doin' both those jobs and drivin' the mail up to the folks in the hills twice a week besides.

"As an old newspaperman, I've always been something of a collector of stories about people and places. They call it history in school, but to me it's just news stories about how things used to be. And I have a particular reason to be interested in stagecoach drivers, as I might tell you about later.

"But I guess it was findin' myself drivin' the mail through the Gold Country that really got me thinkin' again about those stage drivers of sixty and seventy years ago. You know, it's rough enough bouncin' up and down these hillsides inside a modern-day automobile—even one that's only a few years old, like my 1916 Model T. But in those days, the mail and the gold and a lot of other important things traveled by stagecoach. And there's no disputin' that folks really looked up to the fellas who drove those coaches—and not just because they were sittin' up on the box, eight feet off the ground!"

Alex waved his hand. "Were they really heroes, though, Mr. Perkins? What was so special about them?"

"Well, now . . ." Mr. Perkins blinked, and Margaret could see little spots of red rise in his cheeks. "Whether they were heroes or not, I'll leave for you to judge. But I can tell you that it was no easy job to drive through the dust and heat of those Gold Country summers, or across rain-swollen creeks and washed-out trails in the winter time!"

"I'm sure you had to be brave and strong to be a stagecoach driver," Miss McCabe said helpfully. "That's why they came to be known as Knights of the Road. Isn't that right, Mr. Perkins?"

"Oh, they were known by many names, 'whips' and 'jehus' bein' two of the favorites. But to me, yep, Knights of the Road is the title that fits them best. You might say they were the glue that stuck these diggings together. Why, without the stage lines, the most reliable transportation would have been on the back of a horse—or a mule, if you had a load to carry. When you've got a fair piece to travel, that can be a little rough on your backside, believe me!

"And the stages carried more than just people lookin' to get rich quick. The drivers brought news from all the places they visited, and beyond. 'Course, they also carried the thing that made this part of our fair state the talk of the land—gold!

"But most important of all was the mail. You know, the miners were down on their luck a good part of the time. And when things were lookin' grim, it was those letters from home that cheered 'em up and kept 'em chasin' that rainbow. Here, let me show you something."

Stooping down to open his satchel, Mr. Perkins pulled out a brown leather pouch and held it up for the class to see. "I've been collectin' some mementos of that time, and I brought a few along in case you'd be interested. This here pouch was used to hold the mail. See how the leather's cracked? This bag must have traveled thousands of miles bringin' news back and forth between the camps and the out-side world. Here, why don't you pass it around and have a look at it."

"I like the smell," Alex said as he took the pouch from Mr. Perkins. "Hey, what's this inside?" Reaching into the pouch, he took out a crusty yellowish rock about the size of a peanut shell. "Whatever it is, it's heavy," he said, weighing it in his palm.

Mr. Perkins chuckled. "That, son, is what brought all those folks runnin' when the Gold Rush exploded on these empty hills."

"Gold?" Alex yelped as the other children left their seats and crowded around to look. "Real gold?"

"Real gold it is," Mr. Perkins nodded. "It may not look like much, but to those hard-workin' miners, a nugget like that was just about the prettiest sight in the world."

"I've got something else to show you," Mr. Perkins resumed when everyone had finished looking at the gold nugget. "Since you're all standin' anyway, why don't you come gather round Miss McCabe's desk so we can look at it together." Rummaging in his satchel, he fished out a large map and unfolded it carefully on top of the teacher's desk.

"You see, we can't even begin to talk about stage-coachin' without talkin' about our capital city. Now, Sacramento wasn't the capital of California when the Gold Rush started, but to the men in these parts it surely was the stage-coach capital of the territory. Can you see why?"

Jimmy bent over the map. "Looks to me like there were plenty of other towns that were close to the mines," he said.

"Yes, there were," Mr. Perkins agreed. "But what do you see that would make Sacramento the hub of activity hereabouts?"

"Look carefully at the geography," Miss McCabe suggested when no one ventured a guess.

"Is it because of the rivers?" Pablo asked uncertainly.

"You're partly right," answered Mr. Perkins. "Look at this." He traced the path of the Sacramento River with a finger. "See how the Sacramento runs right down to Suisun and San Pablo Bays? And right here is San Francisco Bay. That means the river towns, including Sacramento, had a straight shot down to 'Frisco and the Pacific Ocean.

"And by golly those old paddle-wheelers and other vessels that traveled that waterway made mighty good use of it, too. Over the years thousands of gold hunters came to the Sierras by way of San Francisco and the Sacramento River. Of course, for most of those men, that was just the last part of a journey that lasted for months. From all over the world they came, from back East here in the States, and from Europe, and South America—"

"And Mexico, like my grandfather," Pablo interrupted.

"And don't forget China!" added Jimmy. "My grandfather came on a big boat all the way across the Pacific Ocean. My father says many Chinese came to work on the railroads, and later Chinese miners worked hard to get more gold out of places that the old miners weren't using any more."

"That's exactly right," Mr. Perkins agreed. "So you can imagine that Sacramento was quite a bustlin' place even in those days! Why, old-timers say it was often as lively in the wee hours of the morning as it was at midday. When one of those big steamboats tied up along the riverbank, the men whooped and hollered and hustled down the gangplank headin' for the hotels and the stage offices, and—if Miss McCabe doesn't mind my sayin' so—for the saloons and gamblin' halls, too."

"Mr. Perkins, you keep saying 'men,'" Margaret pointed out. "Weren't there some women passengers too? And children?"

Peter rolled his eyes. "Of course there weren't, Margaret. Mining and panning aren't *women's* work."

"What do you know, Smarty?" Margaret replied hotly. "When we learned about the pioneers coming west, Miss McCabe said the women worked right alongside the men."

"I've heard that about the pioneers also," Mr. Perkins said. "But I must admit that women and children were scarce in California mining towns, at least in the early days. When women did come through, it was often as travelin' entertainers, like the famous dancer Lola Montez and her young friend, Lotta Crabtree. Little Lotta was a huge success—so much so that she went on to have quite a career as a singer and a dancer. And it all started right here in the gold fields.

"But mostly it was a man's world until some people settled down and began raisin' families. Remember, a lot of

17

the gold seekers didn't come here to stay. They left their families hopin' for a quick strike and plannin' to head back for wherever they came from if fortune smiled on them."

"See?" Peter said smugly. Margaret stuck out her tongue at him.

"Of course, I'm sure it would've been a *better* place if more womenfolk *had* been around," Mr. Perkins added hastily.

"Perhaps you can get back to telling us about Sacramento," Miss McCabe suggested.

"Yes, well, hrrmph. As I was sayin', Sacramento was bustin' with activity back then. Imagine the scene, if you can. It's not even daybreak yet, and a big San Francisco steamer is pullin' up alongside the shore. Maybe a hundred stagecoaches or more are linin' the streets, waitin' to take the men up to the Gold Country. Places like the Orleans Hotel are all lit up by lanterns and brimmin' with men rushin' about, talkin' different languages and tryin' to keep track of their belongings as the luggage is stowed away or strapped onto the tops of the coaches. All the while, wild-eyed horses are snortin' and pawin' the ground, waitin' for the brake to be eased and the driver's whip to crack.

"Soon everyone's tryin' to clamber aboard at once, and the stage drivers are hollerin' out the names of the stops they'll be makin'." Mr. Perkins cupped his hands to his mouth. "All aboard for Fiddletown," he called. "And Angel's Camp, Whiskey Slide, Rattlesnake Bar, and Bear Valley!"

"What strange names!" Margaret giggled.

"Yeah, how come they had such funny names?" Alex piped up.

Mr. Perkins smiled. "Now, that's a fascinating subject for an old news hound like me. You see, up here in Gold Country it seems that most every place gold was found—and some places it wasn't—has a name with a story behind it. In some cases, the name practically tells the story all by itself." He tapped the map with a finger. "Take Fiddletown, for instance. How do you suppose that little settlement got its name?"

"Because it was started by somebody named Fiddle?" Jimmy guessed.

"No, not quite," Mr. Perkins answered, "though that's a good guess. The way I heard it, Fiddletown was settled by people from Missouri who enjoyed fiddle music. They were always fiddlin', or so people said. So somebody suggested they should call the place Fiddletown. That's about all it took.

"As a matter of fact, you can tell quite a bit about the history of these parts from the names the men gave to their new homes. Maybe after I'm gone you and Miss McCabe can try to figure out the stories behind names like Hangtown, Tin Cup, Sorefinger, Frogtown, Liar's Flat, and—my favorite—Squabbletown."

"Squabbletown might be a good name for Manchester School," Miss McCabe observed wryly.

"What about Manchester?" Peter inquired. "How did this one-horse place get its name?"

"It wasn't always a 'one-horse place,' Peter," said Miss McCabe. "Back in the old days, Manchester School could barely hold all the children who lived here."

"It sure has shrunk, then," said Pablo. "Is that because all the gold was found?"

"I'm afraid that's so," nodded Mr. Perkins. "People do have a way of movin' on when the gold gives out. As to how the town got its name, I did hear a story about that.

"One day back when the town was a thrivin' settlement, a big, burly blacksmith by the name of Chester got into a terrible scrap with one of the miners. As the fight wore

20

on, these two mountain men attracted a sizable crowd. Chester was rather enjoyin' the fray when suddenly he realized that one of his thumbs had been half chawed through! At that point he figured enough was enough, and with one mighty blow he laid the miner out cold on the hard ground.

"Well, it seems that one admiring witness to this little fracas remarked, 'Some man, that Chester!' And, accordin' to the tale, from then on the blacksmith's town was known as Manchester."

Margaret wrinkled her nose. "His thumb was half chewed! Is that the sort of thing that went on back then?"

"I'm afraid those were rather rough 'n ready times," Mr. Perkins answered. "In fact, that's the name of another gold town—Rough and Ready. Nobody's ever accused those gold-seeking types of being overly civilized, I don't suppose. And you know what people say, Miss—boys will be boys."

"Enough about Manchester!" Jimmy broke in. "You haven't told us yet why the stagecoach drivers were so special. Were they real heroes, like Miss McCabe said?"

"Well, now, I suppose the word 'hero' means different things to different people," Mr. Perkins said thoughtfully. "I'll tell you what. Now that we're done lookin' at the map, why don't you all sit back down for a spell and I'll tell you a few tales about the Knights of the Road. As I said before, then you can decide for yourselves whether or not they deserve to be called heroes."

"I don't know who you young'uns would consider a hero," Mr. Perkins began when the students were all seated again. "In this day of motor coaches and newfangled flying machines, a stagecoach driver might not seem so special to you. But in the 1850s, they were the kings of the road. Back then, everyone sat up and took notice when a team of horses came thunderin' into a stage stop, pullin' a fancy Concord Coach."

"Concord Coach, what's that?" asked Alex.

"The best danged coach ever built, that's what! Why, the Concord could out-perform anything on four wheels. And they were a dazzling sight, too, with bright red bodies and sometimes a scene painted on each door. The Concord was so well-built that passengers rode in comfort even over roads that were filled with rocks and ruts. I guess you all know about Mark Twain, don't you?"

"Sure, he wrote *Tom Sawyer* and *Huckleberry Finn,*" Pablo said.

"And a lot of other good stories, too," Mr. Perkins added. "That is, when he wasn't newspaperin' or nosing around the gold fields. Well, Mr. Mark Twain called the Concord a 'cradle on wheels.' They weren't like Model T's that are put together in some big factory. They were made by hand by skilled craftsmen who took pride in every last detail.

"Anyhow, as I was sayin', all the work in town came to a halt when the Knights of the Road arrived in their fancy Concords. Dressed in their mountain finery—some of 'em sportin' the finest hats, gloves, and boots that money could buy— well, those jehus were the envy of all who gazed upon 'em. Yes, sir, when they jumped down from the box and swaggered toward the hash house to get some grub, bystanders opened a path for 'em. People felt privileged just to eat at the same table with a stagecoach driver—and they wouldn't think of takin' a bite until he was served."

"But when I referred to them as heroes," Miss McCabe interrupted, "I was thinking of the conditions of the roads and all the dangers they must have faced. Goodness, even today it can be impossible to drive through the mountains during the winter months. If a modern automobile can't make it over those roads, what must it have been like for a stagecoach?"

"Oh, it was risky and dangerous, there's no doubtin' that," Mr. Perkins answered. "But those drivers were a hearty breed, and they were accustomed to matchin' wits with Mother Nature. Nowadays anybody who can afford an automobile can learn to drive one, but drivin' stages—that was an art. Believe me, it wasn't a job for everyone!"

"Especially not *girls*," Peter said, tugging at one of Margaret's pigtails.

Margaret blushed. "Oh, that's right, Peter," she said sarcastically, swinging round to glare at him. "Girls are much too weak and dainty—aren't they, Mr. Perkins? They can't do he-man things like gamble their family's money away and chew off people's thumbs."

Mr. Perkins's eyes twinkled. "I'd be the last to say what a girl or woman can or can't do, Miss. Remember, I took over my job from Mrs. Clampett, and people tell me that even in her seventies she was a mighty skilled driver as well as a keen banker!

"But man or woman, you'll have to admit that a stage driver's job wasn't for everybody. It took some doin' to guide a big stage along a ribbon of road that had been carved out of a mountain cliff—especially in the dark, with rain or snow comin' down and gusts of wind threatening to blow the coach right off the mountain! It was no picnic, either, tryin' to pull a fully loaded stage out of a muddy creek bottom after it had sunk up to its axles in goo and muck. And even when the goin' was good, there was always the unexpected."

"Like what?" asked Jimmy.

"Well, like trees fallin' across the road, or coaches losin' a wheel, or horses throwin' a shoe . . ."

"And sometimes there were bandits," Pablo added. "Right, Mr. Perkins?"

"Yes, and sometimes there were bandits," Mr. Perkins agreed.

"Bandits!" Alex exclaimed. "Real bandits?"

"I'll say they were real," Mr. Perkins replied grimly. "As real as the gold and money and watches and jewelry they made off with!"

"Wow! Tell us about the bandits," pleaded Jimmy.

"I thought you wanted to hear about the stagecoach drivers," Peter reminded him.

"Them, too. But first I want to hear about the bandits! Did they carry guns and wear masks on their faces? What happened to them when they got caught? Did any of them ever get away for good?"

"Whoa, hold your horses," Mr. Perkins laughed. "One question at a time!

"To take your last question first, maybe some bandits were never caught, but there was little mercy for those who were. In those days even a hard-up miner could get himself hung by the neck for makin' off with another fellow's gold dust. And some bandits died in shootouts, either with the people they were tryin' to rob—including some of the stage drivers—or with lawmen. That's what people say happened to two famous marauders of the Gold Country, Joaquin Murrieta and his sidekick, Three-Fingered Jack. Supposedly they met their end in a shootout with the California Rangers. Whatever the truth of the story may be, there's no doubt that many badmen did go to meet their Maker in a blaze of gunfire!"

"Gosh, right here in California?" Alex said wonderingly.

"Right here in California. As for how they went about their dirty business, that was different from one outlaw to another. You take the notorious Black Bart, for example. Now, there was a stagecoach robber with a style all his own. When a coach was travelin' some lonesome stretch of road, Black

Bart would suddenly step out of the brush and order the stage to stop. He was always dressed the same way, in a long, light-colored coat called a duster. But you really knew it was Black Bart from the flour sack he wore over his head, with holes cut in it so he could see. Very politely, he would ask the driver to throw down his treasure box. Of course, he could afford to be polite, since the shotgun he was aimin' left the driver little choice!

"To top it all off, Black Bart was something of a poet! There was a poem he left at the scene of one of his robberies that I know by heart. Would you like to hear it?"

"Yes, tell us," Jimmy begged.

"All right, listen carefully now. It goes like this:

*Here I lay me down to sleep*
*To wait the coming morrow,*
*Perhaps success, perhaps defeat,*
*And everlasting sorrow.*
*Let come what will I'll try it on,*
*My condition can't be worse;*
*And if there's money in that box*
*'Tis money in my purse!"*

"Hey, that's pretty nifty!" Alex said. As Miss McCabe frowned, he added hurriedly, "I mean, for a bandit."

"He doesn't sound like such a happy man," Margaret remarked. "What happened to him in the end?"

"I guess you could say that it was sorrow he found," Mr. Perkins answered. "Black Bart robbed more than twenty-five coaches before he was finally caught and unmasked. The amazin' thing was, Black Bart turned out to be a well-known gentleman in San Francisco society! He'd been living a kind of double life, you might say. Anyway, what happened to him after he served his time in San Quentin prison, no one knows. For a while he went back to San Francisco, but naturally he couldn't live the same life as before. Eventually the

old man wandered off into the towns of the San Joaquin Valley and wasn't heard from again."

Miss McCabe cleared her throat. "Mr. Perkins, I'm sure everyone is enjoying your accounts of colorful criminals, but I think we might also like to hear about some of those heroes we were promised."

"Yes, ma'am," Mr. Perkins said sheepishly. "I do tend to get sidetracked a bit."

"That's okay!" Jimmy said. "You can get sidetracked all you want."

"Especially if it means no 'rithmetic today," Peter whispered to Pablo.

"Well, I'll try to do a better job of stickin' to my subject," Mr. Perkins smiled. "The trouble is where to start. There were so many outstanding drivers I could tell you about. Probably the best-known of the bunch was a fella by the name of Hank Monk. He wasn't necessarily the best, but his name became well-known because he happened to take a famous passenger on a hair-raisin' ride over the Sierras—a man named Horace Greeley, who was a publisher and editor from the East. That trip became the talk of the territory. Later on a couple of writers, including Mark Twain, wrote about it, and that pretty well guaranteed the fame of Mr. Monk.

"Another famous California whip was John Reynolds, though he worked mostly in the southern part of the state. He was such a popular figure that people said he knew every man, woman, and child in the city of Los Angeles! And then there was Dave Berry, who was described as the oldest whip in California. It was Berry who established a record I shudder to think of—it's said he rode half a million miles in his career on the box! That's an awful lot of jostlin' and joltin', if you ask me.

"Oh, yes, there were many fine whips. One who was ranked with the best of 'em was a black man, George Monroe. He spent a lot of his drivin' career on a difficult and dangerous run that went through Yosemite Valley. If you've ever been there, you know that Yosemite is one of the natural wonders of the world. For that reason, it attracted visitors from faraway places, and Monroe found himself with the safety of some pretty important people in his hands—including a couple of presidents of the United States."

"How about the drivers who worked around here?" Alex asked. "Were any of them famous?"

"You bet!" Mr. Perkins answered. "One of 'em was 'Uncle Jim' Miller, who got his drivin' education on the steep roads of the Sierra. Besides being recognized as a top driver, he was known for the huge nine-pound silver watch he carried—and for the number of times his stage was held up by bandits like Black Bart.

"But there's one Gold Country driver whose story is the most amazin' of all. Charley Parkhurst was his name, but he was known far and wide as One-Eyed Charley. I like to call him the California Whip, because even though there were many outstanding jehus, Charley was something special. His story has it all—spine-tinglin' rides, holdups by bandits, stagecoach racin', and lots more. Why, I could tell you tales about Charley—goodness gracious!" Mr. Perkins grimaced as the school buzzer sounded loudly. Margaret couldn't help giggling as the banker clapped his hands over his ears.

"Oh, dear, is it lunchtime already?" Miss McCabe said, looking up at the schoolroom clock. "We've all been so involved in your stories that I completely forgot to notice the time. Will you stay and tell us about Charley after lunch?"

"Be glad to," Mr. Perkins mumbled. "If you promise to warn me the next time that danged thing is about to go off."

"Hooray!" Jimmy cried. "More stories!"

"And no 'rithmetic," Peter whispered to Pablo.

"Let's go play drivers 'n bandits!" Alex yelled. With a shout the boys grabbed their lunch pails and ran for the schoolhouse door.

"Hey, wait for me!" Margaret cried as she fished her lunch out of her desk. "I want to play, too!"

"Aw, you can't play, Sis," Alex called over his shoulder. "This is a *boys'* game."

"Yeah, Margaret, a *boys'* game," Peter echoed as he ran out the door. "Girls can't be drivers and bandits, you know."

"Who says they can't?" Margaret yelled furiously, stamping her foot. But the boys were already gone.

# California, Ho!

While the boys spent their lunch hour driving and rob-
bing make-believe stagecoaches, Margaret wandered off by
herself, munching on her sandwich and poking through the
grassy field where she had thrown the baseball during recess.
Every now and then she heard the boys shouting and
stopped to listen to what was going on.

"All right, driver, throw down that box!" she heard Alex
yell in a shrill voice.

"Don't shoot, amigo!" That was Jimmy, pretending to
be Mexican.

With a sigh Margaret finished off her sandwich and
knelt down to part the grass with her hands. "It is *not* fair,"
she muttered, feeling for the ball in the grass.

"That's the last stage you'll ever rob, Black Bart!" That
was Peter, playing the sheriff—naturally. Suddenly Margaret
sat down and burst into tears. "Oh, I wish I were a boy!" she
cried out loud.

"You don't mean that now, do you, Miss?" said a
friendly voice.

Startled, Margaret caught her breath and scrambled to
her feet.

30

"Mr. Perkins! You scared me!"

"Oh, I *am* sorry," the banker apologized. "I didn't mean to sneak up on you. Actually, that makes two things I'm sorry about. I came to say that I'm mighty sad if my tales are causin' you any trouble, because I surely didn't mean for them to."

"Oh, that's okay, Mr. Perkins," Margaret sniffled. "It's not your fault. I suppose the boys are right about drivers and bandits being men. I just wish the history books talked about women and girls once in a while! Didn't women ever do anything exciting?"

"Why, of course they did!" Mr. Perkins exclaimed. "That's not what you're cryin' about, is it? Why, have you forgotten about the pioneers? Or how about—well, now, how about those brave women who helped slaves escape to freedom in the days before the Civil War? You know, women were very important in the movement to end slavery."

"Really?" Margaret asked, trying to smile for Mr. Perkins's sake.

"Of course! Oh, there have been lots of women who did brave things, but oftentimes it was behind the scenes, so to speak. Did you know that during the Civil War there were women on both sides who disguised themselves as men so they could fight? And there were others who risked their lives working as spies, some of 'em for President Abe Lincoln himself. Or how about Elizabeth Cady Stanton? Surely you know about her?"

Margaret shook her head.

"You don't?" Mr. Perkins was astonished. "Why, who do you think was one of the most important people in the movement to get women the right to vote? You know about the right to vote, don't you?"

Margaret nodded. "My mother's all excited because she can vote for President this year. Miss McCabe said it has something to do with changing the Constitution."

"That's exactly right," Mr. Perkins agreed. "The thing is, that didn't happen overnight. No, sir, it was all because of people like Elizabeth Cady Stanton. Now, there was a strong and brave woman! She started out being one of those women who spoke out against slavery. Then, when she stood up and said that women would be like slaves until they had the same right to vote as men, she was made the laughingstock of the town. That was back in 1848 or so, when hardly anyone could imagine such a thing. That didn't stop her, though. She just plain refused to give up—and now here it is 1920, and her dream has finally come true."

"But the boys don't pay any attention to those things," Margaret complained as she brushed the grass off her dress. "And anyway, it's still the men who get to be the generals and presidents and sheriffs and—well, whatever is brave and exciting. It isn't fair!

"And look at me, Mr. Perkins. Here I am crying, which you'd never see Peter do in a million years—not in front of anybody, anyhow. Why do girls have to be different?"

"Well, now, let's think about that," Mr. Perkins said as he took Margaret by the elbow and began to lead her back toward the schoolhouse. "Which do you think calls for more bravery—to show how you feel when you're happy or when you get hurt, right out in public, or to hide everything behind a poker face so nobody knows your true feelings? Did it ever occur to you that sometimes menfolk might be *scared* of showin' how they feel?"

"I never thought of it that way," Margaret admitted.

"Well, that's how it is, often enough," Mr. Perkins said. "Why, I'm willin' to guess some of those boys are a wee bit scared of *you*, not wantin' to admit you can do some things as well as they can! Anyhow, I think you should be mighty proud of standin' up for yourself and sayin' how you feel, especially when you're outnumbered the way you are. Say, what's this?"

Bending down, Mr. Perkins reached into the grass and plucked out Margaret's baseball. "Well, I'll be," he said. Looking through the trees toward the front of the schoolhouse, he measured the distance with his eyes. "Miss," he said, handing Margaret the ball, "that was one powerful throw!"

"Thanks, Mr. Perkins," Margaret smiled, wiping away her tears. "I feel better now. Oh-oh, there's the buzzer. We'd better get inside."

"Just one thing more," the banker said. "That tale I'm fixin' to tell this afternoon, about One-Eyed Charley—I'd like you to pay special attention to it. I think you might find it interesting."

"Sure, Mr. Perkins," Margaret shrugged. "Please don't think I don't like your stories. They're nifty, honest!"

"I'm glad you think so," Mr. Perkins replied, patting her on the shoulder. "But take it from me, the tale of One-Eyed Charley is the 'niftiest' of 'em all!"

A few minutes later, the five children of Manchester School were back in the schoolhouse, waiting eagerly for Mr. Perkins to resume his stories.

"Psst! Margaret! Ask lots of questions," Peter hissed as Margaret slipped into her seat. "That way we won't have any 'rithmetic tests today."

"I don't care if we *do* have a test," Margaret answered stiffly. "*I'm* ready for mine."

"Smartypants!"

"It's better than being dumb, like some people!"

"Children!" Miss McCabe tapped her pointer on her desk. "If we can all settle down now, Mr. Perkins can continue with his talk.

"Mr. Perkins, I believe you were going to tell us about a driver called One-Eyed Charley, is that right?"

"Ahem . . . Yes, that's correct, ma'am," Mr. Perkins answered as he took his place at the front of the room. With a wink at Margaret, he went on, "I said this morning that I had a special reason to be interested in stagecoach drivers. Well, that reason was Charley. You see, he was the only famous Gold Country whip I had the pleasure of knowin' personally."

"Gee, you mean you were alive during the Gold Rush?" Alex interrupted. "You don't look *that* old."

"Oh, Alex," Margaret murmured, looking in dismay at Mr. Perkins. To her surprise, he burst out laughing.

"Well, son, that's very observant of you," said Mr. Perkins. "The fact is, I wasn't suggestin' that *I* was around to witness the Gold Rush. You see, by the time I met Charley, he had been retired from drivin' for a number of years. He was an old man livin' with his memories in a little cabin near a town called Watsonville, down by Monterey Bay. I was still in my teens then, and livin' with my family on my father's farm.

"But we're gettin' ahead of our story. Let's begin at the beginnin', with the long-ago year of 1812, when these United States were still a new country, and to most folk California was an unknown place clear across the frontier. That's when Charley was born, in a place called Lebanon, in the state of New Hampshire. Anybody know where that is?"

"I do," Pablo said. "It's on the other side of the United States."

"That's right," Mr. Perkins said with a nod. "If I'm not mistaken, part of it even touches the Atlantic Ocean.

"Unfortunately, Charley's early years weren't happy ones. He was abandoned when he was just a little tyke and grew up not knowin' his parents. Instead he ended up spendin' most of his time in an orphanage. Everybody know what that is?"

Margaret raised her hand. "It's a place for children who don't have parents to take care of them," she said.

"Right again," Mr. Perkins agreed. "And I guess you can

imagine that it isn't much fun growin' up without a mother and father to watch over you. I suppose it would be kind of like livin' at school and not bein' able to leave."

"Yuck!" exclaimed Alex. "If that happened to me, I'd run away!"

Mr. Perkins chuckled. "Well, you'd have got along with Charley, then, 'cause that's just what he did. One day he decided he'd had enough of orphanage life and it was time to strike out on his own. That took some bravery, because he was only about twelve years old at the time, and he had no place to go and no money except for a pocketful of change he'd earned doin' odd jobs.

"But Charley *was* brave. With nothin' much in the world but the clothes on his back, he slipped out of the orphanage and headed for the nearest stage stop.

"When he got there, he pulled out a good number of his hard-earned coins. Showin' them to the driver, he told him he wanted to go as far as those coins would take him.

"The driver might have guessed that the boy was a runaway, but Charley looked older than his years. Then, too, maybe the driver had ventured out on his own when he was young. That wasn't so unusual in those days. Anyway, he motioned for Charley to climb aboard, sayin' he'd let him know when his miles had run out.

"So Charley hoisted himself into the coach and said goodbye to the orphanage for good. And so began the adventure that would last most of his life."

"Is that how he got to California?" Alex inquired. "Did the driver take him all the way across the country?"

"Oh, my, no," Mr. Perkins smiled. "But Charley did ride that stage clear to another state, as you'll see.

"Now that he was free, for a while Charley couldn't get enough of peerin' out the stage window at the countryside and the little towns they passed through. But the excitement of the day started to catch up with him, and after a few hours the swayin' of the coach began to lull him to sleep. Once his eyes fell shut, nothing could wake him up—not other passengers talkin', or a change of drivers, or the hitchin' up of fresh teams. With a nod and a wink, the first driver told the next one about the sleepin' lad, and the second driver told the one after him, and so it went until the stage rolled to a stop in Worcester, Massachusetts. When the last driver climbed down from the box, he shook Charley awake and told him he'd run out of miles, 'cause they had come to the end of the line.

"Imagine wakin' up in a new place you've never seen before, hungry as a horse and not knowin' a single soul! But nothing stopped Charley. He rubbed his eyes, looked around, thanked the driver, and handed him his coins. Then he jumped down from the coach and set off lookin' for the nearest livery stable."

Margaret felt a tap on her shoulder. "Ask him what a livery stable is," Peter's voice whispered.

"Ask him yourself," she hissed without turning around.

Miss McCabe raised an eyebrow. "Is something the matter?" she inquired, looking directly at Margaret.

"No, ma'am," Margaret blushed. Feeling a poke in her back, she added, "But, um, I was just wondering if Mr. Perkins could explain what a livery stable is. I mean, I know about stables, but what's a livery?"

"Well, in this case the two words go together," Mr. Perkins explained. "Livery stables were places where horses were brought to be fed and cared for—something like horse hotels, I guess you could say. And often they had horses and carriages for hire."

"But why did Charley go there?" Peter whispered. "He didn't have any money to rent a horse."

"How should I know?" Margaret said impatiently and blushed again as she realized she had spoken out loud.

"Did you have another question, Miss?" Mr. Perkins asked, his eyes twinkling.

"No, but Peter does," Margaret answered brightly. "Don't you, Peter?" she asked, turning around and making a face at him.

"Er, well, no, I mean, yes, I guess so. My question is, how he could rent a horse if he spent his money already?"

"Well, now, hang on," Mr. Perkins laughed. "I didn't say he was there to hire a horse. No, he was figurin' on gettin' himself a job. As it turned out, the fellow who owned the stable, a man by the name of Ebenezer Balch, was lookin' for help just then. He wasn't eager to take Charley on at first, because he hadn't had much luck with teenagers. But something in the way Charley carried himself must have convinced him, because after eyeballin' the lad for a spell and askin' some questions, he decided to give him a try. And when he found out that the boy had no home to go to, he let him stay in the back room of the stable besides.

"Ebenezer's gamble turned out to be a wise decision. Not only was Charley a reliable worker, but he also had a way with animals. So everything was workin' out fine for all concerned. Ebenezer had the help he needed, and Charley had a place to live, a job, and a start on the way of life that was to make him famous."

"But if he was working in a stable, when did he start driving stagecoaches?" asked Pablo.

"Yeah, let's get to the exciting part," Jimmy chimed in.

Mr. Perkins held up a hand. "Patience! You don't become a master coachman overnight, you know. First you start with the easy things, like one horse pullin' a wagon or a small carriage. Then, after you get a feelin' for the road and for the critter who's doin' the pullin', you move up a notch.

"It's something like goin' to school, learnin' one thing at a time, like how to count numbers before you get to doin' multiplication and long division. Only Charley's school was the stable, and his teacher was Ebenezer. After he learned how to handle one horse, he moved up to a two-horse team. Then, after lots of practice, he was ready for a four-horse team. Finally, he graduated, so to speak, to workin' with teams of six horses.

"I guess you could say that was something like goin' to college and gettin' straight A's. You see, there weren't a whole lot of fellas who could master drivin' six headstrong horses at once. But after several years, Charley was looked upon as one of the best.

"Then the day came when Ebenezer Balch decided to move on. He sold his livery in Worcester and moved to a town called Providence, in the state of Rhode Island, where he bought two stables. By this time Charley was a skilled coachman, and Ebenezer was glad to take him along.

"Before long, Charley was even better known than he had been back in Massachusetts. If Charley was drivin', people knew they were in for a smooth trip. As a matter of fact, he was said to be the envy of whips up and down the Atlantic states. Rich folk by the dozens demanded him as their driver when they hired a fancy rig, complete with the stable's best six-horse team to haul it.

"Charley had a good life, but after some years he met two men who were to change it forever. They were James Birch and Frank Stevens, and they were the ones who were responsible for bringing Charley to California."

Walking over to Alex's desk, Mr. Perkins held up the gold nugget he had shown the children earlier.

"It all started with this," he resumed. "When word hit the East that gold had been found in California, it was like a fever came raging through. Thousands of men left their homes and their farms or jobs and headed west, hopin' to

38

strike it rich. Birch and Stevens were two of 'em. But unlike many of the Forty-Niners, they worked at trades other than minin'. You see, the Gold Rush was creating a need for many kinds of businesses, and one of 'em was stagecoachin'.

"Eventually Birch and Stevens helped to form the California Stage Company. The company was a great success, and Jim Birch knew they needed more good drivers. So he sent word back to Charley that he'd pay his way west if Charley would come and drive stages for them in California.

"Well, when it came to chasin' rainbows, Charley was no different from other folks. He didn't need much coaxin' to say goodbye to his friends and the world he knew, and follow the Forty-Niners to the land of plenty."

As Mr. Perkins paused to take a sip of water, Margaret idly scratched some numbers on a slip of paper. Frowning, she raised her hand.

"Mr. Perkins," she said when he looked her way, "if Charley was born in 1812, he was getting close to forty years old when the Gold Rush started. But you haven't said anything about his family. Did his wife come with him? And did he have children?"

"Well, now, those are good questions," Mr. Perkins replied. "The fact is, Charley never mentioned anything about a family in the times I talked with him. Even as an old man, he lived by himself in a small cabin. According to the stories about him, that's always how it was. That's one of the reasons I used to go see him from time to time, along with a younger friend of mine I'll tell you about presently.

We both felt sorry for the old man, even if he himself never complained of bein' lonesome.

"But you mustn't think that bein' a loner meant that he didn't know how to have a good time. In his drivin' days, he could whoop it up with the best of 'em. After he finished a run, as often as not you'd find him in a saloon, tradin' tall tales with other drivers, arguin' politics, playin' poker, and rollin' dice for his cigars. That was the way of life for a Knight of the Road—hard drivin' followed by hard playin', and a lot of tale-spinnin' along the way!

"That's why it's sometimes hard to separate the truth from all the stories that got passed around. Those yarns just kept getting a little bigger with every telling. And more tales were told and retold about Charley Parkhurst than most any other driver in California. After he died, and I started hearin' all those amazin' stories, I kicked myself for not talkin' to him more while I had the chance."

"What was so amazing?" Jimmy asked impatiently. "All you've told us so far is that he was a really good driver. Is that why he was so famous?"

"And you said his story had everything in it, like adventures and bandits," Pablo reminded him.

"Yeah, tell us about holdups and shootouts and stuff like that!" cried Alex.

"All right, all right," Mr. Perkins laughed. "I was coming to that anyhow, because it was shortly after Charley arrived in California that his stage was ambushed."

"Ha! Welcome to Gold Country!" Pablo exclaimed.

"Welcome to Gold Country, indeed," said Mr. Perkins. "That first experience taught Charley a few things about life in these rough 'n ready parts—one of them bein' that he'd have to have a gun handy from then on. But you only had to teach Charley something once, as I'll tell you.

"There are a number of stories about that first ambush. Accordin' to the most popular account, it happened on a narrow stage road that was cut into the side of a mountain. Charley was guidin' his team around a sharp curve, and he slowed 'em to a crawl. Just when he figured he'd made it safely around the bend, he got the surprise of his life.

"Standin' in the way of the stage was a masked highway-man wearin' some kind of sack-like coverings on his feet. The bandit pointed a rifle straight at Charley's belly and told him to throw down the strongbox that carried the gold.

"Charley hesitated a minute, calculatin' his chances of gettin' away without givin' up the box. But he was unarmed, and he knew that even if the bandit's bullet missed, a rifle shot would spook the horses and send the stage tumblin' over the edge of the cliff. Seein' that he had no choice, he grabbed the strongbox from under his seat and tossed it to the ground.

"Oh, but he was mad as a hornet! 'I'll be ready for ya next time!' he yelled as the bandit stepped aside. Spittin' a stream of tobacco juice right at the outlaw, he cracked his whip and lit out for the next stop.

"When he got there, he reported the holdup to the sheriff and described the bandit's red kerchief and the strange wrappings on the man's feet. Hearing Charley's description, the sheriff looked knowingly at his deputy and muttered, 'Sounds like Sugarfoot has struck again.'"

"Sugarfoot!" Alex echoed. "Why would a bandit be called Sugarfoot?"

"Well, now, think about that a minute," Mr. Perkins answered. "What did I just tell you about the bandit that was unusual?"

Alex frowned. "You mean the things he was wearing on his feet?"

"Now you've got it," Mr. Perkins nodded. "Can you guess why those strange wrappings would lead him to be called Sugarfoot?" One by one the children shook their heads. Suddenly Margaret raised her hand.

"You said they were like sacks," she said excitedly. "Were they sugar sacks?"

"Bravo!" Mr. Perkins grinned. "That's exactly what they were."

"But why would a bandit wear sugar sacks on his feet?" Jimmy objected. "That sounds silly to me."

"Maybe it was to disguise his tracks," Pablo suggested.

"But wouldn't he trip over them when he ran away?" Jimmy replied.

"The fact is, I don't know what his reasons were," Mr. Perkins said with a shrug. "But I do know he wasn't goin' to be needin' those sacks much longer."

"How come?" asked Alex. "Did the sheriff get him?"

"No, not the sheriff. Remember when I said that you only needed to teach Charley something once?"

"You mean Charley got him?" Jimmy exclaimed.

"He sure did! You see, it seems that after he was robbed the first time, Charley bought himself a six-shooter. And when he wasn't drivin' stages or whoopin' it up at the local saloon, he was out in the woods practicin' his draw and shootin' at targets. Before long, he got to be a pretty fair gunman, or so they say.

"Well, some months after the first holdup, Sugarfoot decided to try his luck again. Only this time, his luck had run out, 'cause ol' Charley was ready for him. When Sugarfoot demanded the strongbox, Charley leaned over to reach for it and came up with his gun spittin' fire!

"Seein' Sugarfoot stagger, Charley didn't even wait to watch him fall. With a holler that must've shook the rattlesnakes right out of their lairs, he lit out for the next camp. He told his story to the sheriff, who rounded up a posse and headed for the scene.

"As it turned out, the sheriff didn't need the posse. All they found by the side of the road was a dead man wearin' a red kerchief over his face and sugar sacks on his feet."

"Three cheers for old Charley!" Jimmy cried. "Is that how he got to be famous?"

"Oh, that's only a small part of Charley's story," Mr. Perkins replied. "And he was much more famous for his drivin' than for his shootin'.

"The fact is, even though another road agent or two made the mistake of testin' him, Charley didn't much care for shootin' people. He figured there were better ways to deal with the varmints."

"Like what?" asked Pablo. "What could he do with a gun pointed at him?"

"Did he run over them with his stage?" Alex guessed.

Mr. Perkins grinned. "No, but you're close! And the answer does have to do with Charley's special way of handlin' his horses and knowin' how they would react in any situation.

"For instance, there was the time another badman stepped in front of Charley's team as he slowed 'em down to round a bend. This time there was no cliff on the side of the road. When the bandit called for the strongbox, Charley thought fast. Quicker than lightnin', he worked the reins in such a way that the horse nearest the gunman reared up. That knocked the would-be robber to the ground and sent his rifle flyin'." Mr. Perkins chuckled. "By the time the road agent rolled out of the way of the coach's wheels and grabbed his gun, the stage was out of range. Laughin' to himself, Charley went merrily on his way with his strongbox safe beside him.

"And that wasn't the only way Charley had of dealin' with bandits. There was another incident that took place up around Grass Valley. Accordin' to the story, Charley was guidin' his team around some mud holes when a highway-man suddenly appeared from behind a big rock and ordered him to stop. Without even slowin' down, Charley struck out with his whip and lashed the fellow across the eyes!"

"Yow!" Alex exclaimed. "That must have stung!"

"You can bet it did," Mr. Perkins responded. "Howlin' in pain, the road agent dropped his gun and clutched his face. Meanwhile Charley aimed some tobacco juice in his direction and kept right on goin'."

"Wow, Charley sure could think fast," Jimmy observed.

"That he could," agreed Mr. Perkins. "And bein' such a skilled driver, he could handle a whip even better than a gun!"

"Is that why the drivers were called 'whips'?" asked Margaret.

"Well, it wasn't from whippin' bandits, if that's what you mean," Mr. Perkins said. "But it's true that a whip was a tool of the drivin' trade, a kind of symbol of the profession. Here, let me show you." Reaching into his satchel, Mr. Perkins brought out a long black whip. "This is a whip like the one Charley favored, a blacksnake whip. If Miss McCabe doesn't mind, I'll show you how it was used."

Miss McCabe's eyes opened wide in alarm. "You mean, right here?" she asked.

"Sure," Mr. Perkins answered with a grin. "I'm not nearly as good as one of those old drivers, but I've practiced a bit in my time."

"Well . . . if you're careful," Miss McCabe said doubtfully.

"Oh, I'll be careful! I have great respect for a driver's whip, I assure you.

"Here's what we'll do. I'll just stand in the middle of the room, like so. Now you children go stand in the front, two by two, like you're a team of horses. Miss McCabe, you can stand next to the little lady. That gives us a nice six-horse team. Everybody face front now, with your backs to me. You're a team of horses, remember, so you can't see the driver."

Giggling nervously, the children did as they were told.

"Be careful of the lights," Miss McCabe called in a quavering voice.

"Don't you worry," Mr. Perkins answered. "Just keep lookin' toward the front. That's good.

"Now, what a lot of people don't know is that a stage driver would never use his whip to punish his team. No, sir, a gentle touch on their backs was all it took, or just the sound of the whip cracklin' over their heads—like this!" Suddenly Margaret felt a whoosh of air and a loud *crack!* over her head. "Heeyah!" yelled Mr. Perkins, and burst out laughing as Miss McCabe and the other "horses" nearly jumped out of their shoes.

"Gracious!" cried Miss McCabe, ducking her head.

"Can we sit down now?" pleaded Alex, whose eyes were shut tight.

"Hee-hee, sure you can," Mr. Perkins laughed. "I didn't really mean to scare you. You sit back down, and I'll pass the whip around so you can have a look at it. But don't anyone try any tricks with it, 'cause you're likely to put somebody's eyes out."

"Whew, that was scary," Alex said as the children gratefully returned to their seats.

"*I* wasn't scared," Peter boasted.

"You jumped, too!" Margaret said accusingly.

"Did not!" Peter responded indignantly.

"Did too!" retorted Margaret.

"I think we *all* jumped a little," Miss McCabe interrupted. Taking the whip from Mr. Perkins, she fingered the long lash thoughtfully. "And I can see why the whip would be effective even if it never touched the horses."

"Yes, and a skilled driver like Charley could do magical things with it, too," Mr. Perkins observed.

"What do you mean, magical?" asked Pablo.

"Well, as you can see just from lookin' at it, a whip like this is no easy thing to handle. Yet I've heard tell of jehus who could flick a fly off the ear of their lead horse without the horse even knowin' it!" With a wink at Margaret, Mr. Perkins continued, "There was another trick of theirs you might enjoy hearin' about. It was one they reserved for the boys of the minin' camps. You see, it seems that a favorite pastime of these young'uns was to sneak a free ride on the backside of the coaches as they made their way out of town. They'd wait until the stage was about ready to go, and then climb on the back and cling to the rear boot straps, out of sight of the driver.

"'Course, this was against the rules of the stage companies—and dangerous, too. So, when the driver suspected he was carryin' a little extra baggage, he began limberin' up his whip. Then, without even layin' eyes on the culprits, he'd whisk the lash back just enough to serve as a little warnin', you might say. Those boys would let go pronto, I can tell you!"

"I can believe *that*," Jimmy said feelingly, remembering how the whip crackled overhead during Mr. Perkins's demonstration.

"Hmm," murmured Miss McCabe, turning the whip over in her hand. "So they used it to control the boys, did they?"

"Oh-oh," said Pablo. "Something tells me we'd better be good from now on."

With a smile, Miss McCabe carefully laid the blacksnake whip on her desk. "I think we'll just keep this out of harm's way," she told Mr. Perkins.

"Let's get back to Charley," Margaret suggested. "What else did he do that made him famous?"

"Oh, there were quite a number of things, Miss. As I was tellin' you before, those drivers were thought of as pretty special, and if one of 'em could do something better and quicker than the others, then he became something of a celebrity."

"You mean like shooting bandits?" Alex asked.

"No, son, gunnin' down bandits was an added bonus, and it only happened once in a while. The jehus were judged most by things that were part of their everyday job, like controllin' their teams, bravin' storms in the Sierras, and handlin' emergencies.

"And those drivers didn't mind showin' off a little bit, I must say. That was one of the reasons things would come to a halt when the stage came highballin' into town. 'Course, the drivers knew there would be miners and other folk linin' the streets, waitin' to see who and what the stage was bringin' in that day. Knowin' there would be an audience, those whips would put on quite a show, let me tell you! And old Charley was every bit as good as drivers who were much younger than he was—and proud of it, too.

"One of the stunts he and the other drivers used to pull involved the coins people would toss into the road—coins like this three-dollar gold piece I brought along to show you." Reaching into his satchel, Mr. Perkins took out a gold coin and held it between his thumb and forefinger so the children could see it.

"Why did people throw their money in the road?" asked Jimmy.

"I'm comin' to that," Mr. Perkins answered. "It was a kind of a game—a test of skill. Picture yourself sittin' up on the box of the stage, seein' a coin this size lyin' in the road. It wouldn't look very big, would it?"

Jimmy shook his head.

"Well, then, imagine rollin' into town at breakneck speed, kickin' up dust and rocks, and tryin' to *touch* that coin with the wheel of your stage! That was the game. The driver was supposed to run over as many coins as he could, and then he got to keep all the coins he touched.

"Yessir, that took real skill in handlin' a coach and team. And if the stories can be believed, Charley lined his pockets with a good many coins like this one, because he was better at the game than most anybody else. In fact, since this gold piece came from Charley originally, I like to think it's one he might have won in that very way."

"That coin belonged to Charley?" Jimmy asked. "How did you get it? Did he give it to you?"

"He did for a fact," Mr. Perkins nodded. "He gave me a whole bag full of coins, though how that happened is something I'll explain a little later. I have in mind that we might play a little game of our own, with this here gold piece bein' the prize." Mr. Perkins grinned at Jimmy as he laid the gold piece on Miss McCabe's desk. "So pay attention, son, because the game has to do with something that concerns the story of Charley Parkhurst."

"I will!" Jimmy promised. "Wow—just think! A real gold coin!"

Margaret waved her hand. "Mr. Perkins, you said something about emergencies that happened. Besides bandits, what other kinds of emergencies did Charley get into?"

"Oh, I'm sure there were lots of 'em," Mr. Perkins answered. "But there was one tale that followed Charley around his entire career. Everywhere he went, it seemed folks had heard the story—and to many people, it was the one that made him a hero."

"Tell us!" pleaded Jimmy.

"I was just about to," Mr. Perkins said. "That is, if we have time," he added, with a glance at Miss McCabe.

"Oh, I imagine those arithmetic tests I was going to give will keep until tomorrow," the teacher smiled. "That is, if no one minds."

"Hooray!" Jimmy cried.

"Ha! Didn't I tell you?" Margaret heard Peter whisper.

"Just keep the old guy talking, and we won't have to do *anything* today."

"He's *not* old," Margaret whispered fiercely without turning around. Seeing Mr. Perkins looking curiously at her, she gave him a friendly smile. Well, whether he was old or not, he was very nice, she thought. But why had he said that she should pay special attention to Charley's story? And what was the game they were going to play? "Whatever it is, I'm going to try and win," she said to herself. "If *Peter* wins, I'll never hear the end of it." Leaning forward in her seat, she promised herself to listen carefully to the rest of Charley's tale.

# One-Eyed Charley

"As I was sayin'," Mr. Perkins resumed, "this happening I'm about to relate is one that made Charley a hero in the eyes of many people.

"To appreciate this story, you have to imagine one of the worst winters you've ever seen, one where the rain just keeps comin' for weeks on end. In those days, that meant the trails would be washed out—but that didn't stop the stage drivers! No, sir, they'd be out there with their coaches slippin' and slidin' through the mud, tryin' to keep some kind of schedule so the people and the mail and everything else they were carryin' could get through.

"It was just such a winter when this incident occurred. Charley was drivin' through pourin' rain on a run that took him across a narrow bridge on the Tuolumne River. Now, even in dry weather, when the river was low, that bridge was a rickety thing and nothing to brag about. But with all that rain, the water just kept risin' until the river was rushin' down the canyon like a dam had burst. The water was beatin' on the support timbers of the bridge, and it was plain to anybody lookin' at 'em that it was only a matter of time before the supports gave way.

"So when Charley got to the bridge, he pulled his team up and sat there for a spell, studyin' the scene. Then he jumped down from the box and ventured onto the shaky bridge on foot to give it a closer look. The passengers on board the stage must have been sayin' their prayers, seein' the furious water below and their driver walkin' ever so carefully on the bridge, examinin' the supports.

"Well, Charley must have figured his luck had been good up to then, so maybe it would stay good. Anyhow, there was no other way across, and he wasn't the type to turn back and mess up the schedule. So he sloshed back through the rain, nodded to the passengers, and climbed back on the box.

"Very slowly, Charley guided his team onto the bridge, testin' the weight a little at a time until the whole team and coach were on the span. As gently as he could, he urged the animals on.

"And nothing happened—until the lead horses reached the opposite bank. Just then, high up on the box, Charley could feel the bridge startin' to sway underneath him! Knowin' that he and his passengers were seconds away from bein' swept into the raging river, he cracked that blacksnake whip of his and hollered at his team like he'd never hollered before.

"I don't know if the horses could even hear him over the roar of the water and the crackin' of the timbers as the bridge started to go. But those animals felt the bridge movin', and they sensed the whip, and that was all it took. They bolted for the good earth like they'd been shot from a cannon, jerking the coach behind 'em—and not a second too soon! Just as the rear wheels touched solid ground, the timbers gave way, and the bridge collapsed into the water in a thousand pieces.

"As the coach pulled away, you can bet the passengers looked back at the river and said a prayer of thanks. Another couple of seconds, and they would have been in the drink,

bein' swept downriver as helplessly as those shattered pieces of wood.

"Later on, when they got to their destination, those passengers did some serious celebratin'. It didn't take long for that story to travel up and down the Mother Lode, and Charley's daring became the talk of the day."

"Nifty!" Jimmy exclaimed. "No wonder people thought he was a hero."

"Don't forget about the horses," added Margaret. "They were the ones who got everybody out of that fix. They were heroes, too."

Mr. Perkins chuckled. "I suppose you're right, Miss. I imagine Charley was especially good to his team that night, giving 'em extra feed and rubbing 'em down until they were warm and dry, for that was one time the horses saved the day. But there were other times when it was his horses that got him *into* a fix."

"What do you mean, his horses got him into a fix?" Margaret asked. "How could they do that if they always did what he told them?"

"Well, now, Miss, I never said they *always* did as they were told! Horses are beasts, after all, and they've got minds of their own. For instance, there was one happening I remember hearin' about that took place after Charley left the Gold Country. That time, his horses darn near got him killed!"

"After he left?" Pablo repeated. "You mean he drove stages in other places, too?"

"Oh, yes," Mr. Perkins replied. "After leavin' the mountains, Charley drove stages in a number of places around northern and central California. Old-timers say he had runs around San Francisco, and down San Jose way, and over the Santa Cruz Mountains into the area around Monterey Bay. It wasn't just the Gold Country that needed stagecoaches, you know. They were one of the most important means of transportation all through California and the West."

"But what about the time he almost got killed?" Jimmy asked excitedly. "Tell us about that."

"Just like a boy!" Margaret teased. "'Let's hear about some blood!'"

"Well, I hope the story won't disappoint you," Mr. Perkins said with a grin. "As usual, Charley winds up escapin' in the end.

"The incident took place while he was workin' the run from Oakland to San Jose. Charley had just climbed up to the box and hadn't settled in yet when something happened that spooked the horses. I don't know what it was—maybe a gunshot or something like that. Whatever it was, all of a sudden those critters took off runnin' like a pack of hungry grizzlies was on their tails!

"Like I said, Charley wasn't even settled down on the box, though luckily he did have a grip on the reins. But when those horses just sped off without warning, they jerked him clear off the stage! There he was, bein' dragged down the road behind the speedin' animals and about to be run over by his own coach!

"I don't know how he managed to keep his wits about him, but he did. Pullin' on the lines with all his strength, he managed to turn the crazed horses into a thicket by the side of the road. There they got all tangled up in the brush, and that brought the runaways to a stop.

"As you can imagine, the folks on the stage had had the livin' daylights scared out of 'em. Afterward they were so thankful for the way Charley rescued them that they took up a collection and presented him with a hat full of money."

"That's one way to get rich," Peter snickered. "Have lots of accidents!"

Mr. Perkins laughed. "Well, if Charley ever became rich—and I don't know that he did—he must have done it some other way, because his accidents were few and far between. As a matter of fact, it's said that never once in his long drivin' career did a passenger of his get hurt. If that's true, it's an amazin' feat.

"'Course, there was *one* tumble that could have put an embarrassing blemish on that record—except that nobody but Charley was aboard the stage at the time. It happened on the Watsonville run, as I recall, and it's one of the few times in his years as a whip that Charley made a mistake.

"I believe the place was near the hump on Watsonville's old Mount Madonna Road. Wherever it was, Charley confessed to takin' a corner too fast—causin' the stage to tip right over, and sendin' him flyin'!

"That was another time Charley could've been killed. But other than bustin' in his sides—and bustin' up the coach—he came out of the fall in pretty good shape. Before long, he was back on the box. Even gettin' painfully hurt wasn't enough to keep him from doin' what he loved the best."

"Oof!" said Jimmy, holding his sides. "I'll bet he was sore, though."

"I'm sure he was," Mr. Perkins nodded. "But I imagine the aches and pains went away after a while. Unfortunately, I can't say the same for the other time he got seriously hurt. That was one accident that cost him dearly for the rest of his life. The funny thing was, it didn't happen on the road, where you expect danger. Instead, it happened in a blacksmith's shop in a place called Redwood City, between San Francisco and San Jose."

"*What* happened?" Margaret asked anxiously.

"Yeah, don't keep us in suspense!" Jimmy added.

"Did he get burned with a hot iron?" guessed Pablo.

"No, this was another fix that his horses got him into," Mr. Perkins answered. "Or I guess I should say, one horse in particular. It seems that this horse had thrown a shoe, so

Charley was in the blacksmithy fittin' a new one to the horse's hoof. Well, as he was doin' so, that blamed critter kicked Charley square in the face."

"Ouch!" cried Margaret. She felt her stomach turn. "That must have *really* hurt!"

"It did more than that," Mr. Perkins said grimly. "That kick cost Charley his left eye!"

"Ugh," moaned Alex.

"*Ugh* is right," Margaret echoed. "The poor man!"

"Do you really mean he *lost* his eye?" asked Pablo, gulping at the thought.

"Well, not quite," Mr. Perkins said reassuringly. "But that eye never did work right after that. For a time, with his face rearranged somewhat by the horse's kick, people started callin' him Cock-eyed Charley. As you can imagine, that didn't sit too well with him. So he took to wearin' a patch over that eye, which he did for the rest of his life. And before long he had a new nickname, and this one stuck." Bending over, Mr. Perkins rummaged in his satchel. When he straightened up, Margaret was startled to see that he had taken off his glasses and was wearing a black patch over one eye.

"One-Eyed Charley!" Pablo exclaimed.

"That's right, son," Mr. Perkins replied. "From that time on, Charley Parkhurst was known as One-Eyed Charley."

"Gee, I guess everybody knew who One-Eyed Charley was," Pablo remarked as Mr. Perkins took off the eyepatch and returned it to his satchel. "He must've looked different from all the other drivers."

"He did for a fact," answered Mr. Perkins, putting his

glasses on again. "He was the only gun-totin', tobacco-chewin', one-eyed jehu I ever heard of. But Charley would have been recognizable even without the eyepatch. He just looked kind of different. He was rather short and stocky, and unlike some drivers he never grew a beard. He liked to wear pleated shirts that were a bit baggy, and a big, extra-wide belt. And he had a funny habit of wearin' gloves all the time, summer and winter.

"Charley was different in other ways, too. As I told you before, he knew how to have a good time, and yet he was something of a loner. Another thing was that he didn't brag about his adventures like some of the other whips did. He just wasn't one to toot his own horn, I guess. That was true even when I knew him, when he was an old man. I heard more stories about him from other people than from his own lips.

"Still another thing that made Charley different was the interest he took in his passengers. Those drivers were a rough 'n ready breed, but Charley always showed that extra bit of courtesy. If someone needed to get someplace, Charley would find a way to get him there, even if his coach was jam-packed with passengers. He'd climb down from the box, open the stage door, and explain to his fares why the person just had to get to the next stop. By the time he was done, he usually had perfect strangers squeezin' together like they were the best of friends to make room for one more body.

"The same thing went for freight, too. No matter how loaded his coach was, if a parcel or a piece of luggage had to get somewhere, he'd find a way to tie it on or fit it in. They didn't come much tougher than Charley, but they didn't come much nicer, either."

"It's good to know that being strong and courageous can go along with being kind and thoughtful," Miss McCabe observed.

"Yes, and generous, too," Mr. Perkins added. "Maybe because he'd been an almost penniless orphan, Charley liked to help those in need when he could. He wasn't any big spender, but when someone's luck ran out, more than once Charley staked 'em to a new start.

"I even heard about a widow woman who was about to lose her ranch. When Charley got wind of her problem, he dipped into his savings and bought the place. Then he up and gave it to her and her daughter so they wouldn't have to move from their home!

"To top it all off, Charley liked children. They say he even used to give 'em candy when they rode his stage—as legitimate passengers, I mean. Now, that alone made him different from most of the other Knights of the Road."

"My, the afternoon is flying right by," Miss McCabe commented as Mr. Perkins paused to take a drink of water. "If you children have any questions, you'd best ask them before it gets any later."

"I have one," Jimmy said, waving a hand. "Mr. Perkins, what did Charley do after the accident with the horse? He couldn't drive any more, could he? I mean, he would've needed two good eyes to do all that stuff you were telling us about."

"As a matter of fact, he *did* go on driving," Mr. Perkins replied as he set his glass down. "The patch didn't seem to hinder him at all. Maybe it even made him a little more care- ful, though I can't say it stopped him from competin' with the other whips. Even bein' younger and havin' two good eyes, they couldn't outdo old Charley when it came to the stunts those jehus liked to pull."

"You mean like running over coins in the road?" asked Pablo.

"Yes, and racin', too. That was another thing the drivers would get into. Oh, they weren't planned races, with the coaches all lined up at the same starting point. Instead, it would happen this way. Imagine two coaches headin' for the same stop and meetin' somewhere along the way. One driver yells over to the other, and the next thing their passengers know, they're barrelin' along in a furious race to the next stop!"

"I wonder how the passengers felt about suddenly finding themselves in the middle of a wild stagecoach race," Miss McCabe remarked.

"I'll bet they thought it was fun!" Alex said excitedly.

"As a matter of fact, they did." Mr. Perkins's eyes gleamed. "Picture it, if you can! By the time those speedin' coaches reached town, the people on board were screamin' and hollerin', pullin' for their driver to win the race. Oh, it must have been quite a sight, two bright red Concords raisin' clouds of dust as they came barrelin' into town, with their passengers hangin' out the windows and wavin' their hats in the air!

"That was the kind of excitement Charley must have loved, because he kept on with that kind of activity even when he was drivin' down Monterey Bay way and he could barely climb up on the box because his rheumatism was so bad."

"Room-a-what?" asked Alex.

"Rheumatism," Mr. Perkins repeated. "It's a kind of stiffness and pain that gets into the joints and muscles, especially among older folk. You see, by the time Charley was makin' runs down in central California, he was gettin' on in years, especially for a whip.

"But as I said, that didn't stop him from holdin' his own against drivers who were many years younger than he was. If you were a betting man—and a lot of the townfolk did bet on those races—you were smart to put your money on old One-Eyed Charley.

"I once talked to an old codger who remembered seein'

Charley come boomin' into Watsonville, which is near the place my family had its farm. Watsonville lies between San Juan Bautista, the old mission town, and the community of Santa Cruz, which is on Monterey Bay. The run from San Juan Bautista to Santa Cruz was Charley's last hitch, and right up to the end it was the site of some hair-raisin' races.

"See, every so often, Charley's coach would meet the one comin' out of Monterey. With both coaches headed for Watsonville, all it took was for one of those jehus to spy the other's dust—and the race was on! Knowin' the road like the back of his hand, Charley knew when to let his team stretch their legs. By the time they hit the long flat leadin' into town, those Concords would be goin' like there was no tomorrow. Then it was up to people and dogs to get out of the way as best they could!

"Wow, I wish I could have lived in Watsonville then," Jimmy said. "That must have been something to see!"

"That's what the old-timers say," Mr. Perkins agreed. "Long after coach racin' was a thing of the past, they said they'd never seen anything to compare with it.

"But we're nearin' the end of our story now, because by this time the rheumatism was givin' Charley a good deal of pain. He knew he couldn't handle the coach the way he once did. Oh, he was still better than a lot of the younger jehus, but for Charley that wasn't good enough. He didn't want his passengers puttin' their trust in him when he couldn't be as much in charge as he once was.

"So, as hard as it must have been to admit it, the day came when Charley knew he had to hang up his whip."

"Is that when he went to live in the little cabin you told us about?" Margaret asked.

"You have a good memory!" complimented Mr. Perkins. "But that came a bit later. Even if he was through with drivin', Charley wasn't ready to give up stagecoachin' just yet. So for a while he ran his own stage stop out of Santa Cruz.

"The trouble was, that only made him wish he was still drivin'. So then he tried his hand at farmin', workin' a patch of land nearby. He might have done some ranchin' also, and some folk say he even did a bit of loggin' in the forests nearby. In fact, they say he became one of the best lumberjacks around."

"That sounds fishy to me," Pablo objected. "If he was too sore and aching to drive a stage, how could he swing an axe?"

"I think those stories are a little suspect myself," Mr. Perkins admitted. "But I guess they just go to show how much of a legend Charley had become. People were ready to believe he could do most anything.

"But we have Charley's own word that he did some farmin', because that's how he listed himself—as a farmer—when he signed a registration book in Santa Cruz County. That was in the year 1867, when Charley was fifty-five. I once went to see the book myself, and I can tell you it gave me a little thrill to find Charley's signature in it!"

"Registration book?" Margaret asked. "What did he need to sign that for?"

"To show where he lived," Mr. Perkins replied. "And also for registerin' to vote, which Charley did in the elections for United States President in 1868.

"I was four years old then, so naturally I don't remember that election year myself. But I do recall Charley tellin' me about votin' in the first presidential election followin' the Civil War. That was one thing he didn't seem to mind boastin' about—that he'd gone to the trouble to make sure and vote the first chance he got after he retired from stagin'.

"Sometime after that, Charley was finally ready to give up workin' altogether and enjoy a well-earned rest. So he got rid of his place, sold off some cattle he'd been raisin', and moved into a cabin outside Watsonville. That cabin was near the Harmon family, who were friends of his. The Harmons were acquaintances of my family, too, and that was how I met Charley as a teenager. For it was in that cabin, livin' by himself and partly crippled by rheumatism, that One-Eyed Charley Parkhurst spent the rest of his days."

# Charley's Secret

"The poor man!" Margaret exclaimed. "Once he had been so famous, and now he was cooped up in a little cabin all by himself."

"He wasn't always by himself, Miss," Mr. Perkins said consolingly. "He had friends like the Harmons, and he always seemed to enjoy it when the Harmon boy and I used to drop by and sit with him for a spell. Young Harmon and Charley were already fast friends by the time I got to know him. That was in the year 1879, when I was fifteen. And as it turned out, that was Charley's last year on earth.

"The first time I saw him, he was aching and bent from the rheumatism and complainin' about havin' a sore throat. That was one reason I didn't push him into talkin' too much, even though I was burstin' with questions about stage-coachin' and the early days. All the same, he was in pretty good spirits, considerin' the pain he was in.

"Charley still had a soft spot for young folk, I imagine, because when he died, both the Harmon boy and I were in for a surprise. Charley left all his savings to young Harmon. I guess that was his way of sayin' thanks for all the times the boy went to see him at the cabin. And to me he left a small bag of gold coins, including the one I showed you before. That was quite a shock, because I barely knew the old man— and yet he remembered me in his will. That made me doubly sorry I hadn't made more time to visit with him and keep him company."

"You mean you didn't see him very often?" Margaret asked.

"Oh, my, no. I was only up at Charley's cabin a few times. Most days I was busy helpin' out my folks on the farm. Until the last time I saw him, I didn't understand how sick he really was." Mr. Perkins shook his head sadly. "I'll never forget that last visit. It was in the wintertime, and I could see that Charley was a very sick man. He was fightin' not only old age and the rheumatism, but cancer of the tongue as well. He was very weak and couldn't talk much. Fortunately, by that time there was almost always a friend or neighbor watchin' over him. They all knew he was just about around the bend."

Picturing the suffering old man, Margaret felt her eyes sting. "Was someone with him when he died?" she asked in a trembling voice.

"I'm afraid not," Mr. Perkins answered. "The end came a few days after Christmas, when he was alone in his cabin."

"That's not fair!" Margaret protested as her eyes welled with tears. "Charley was one of the best stagecoach drivers ever, and he helped people and saved their lives, and then he died all by himself in a lonely cabin."

"It's like he was an orphan all over again," Pablo remarked.

Mr. Perkins's eyes grew sad. "That's true—and I wish the story had a happier ending. But you must remember that Charley lived a very full life, more so than maybe any of us will. And there's one other thing that may help with the hurt, Miss. You see, as special as Charley's life was, he had a secret that makes it even more special. And maybe the best part of all is that he could keep his secret until the very end. That's the way he wanted it, and maybe he wouldn't have got his wish if he had been surrounded by people or laid up in a hospital."

"What was it?" Margaret asked tearfully. "What was the secret?"

"Well, now, let's see whether you can guess. Remember I said we might play a kind of game?" Walking over to Miss McCabe's desk, Mr. Perkins picked up the three-dollar gold piece.

"As I've told you, this here is one of the coins Charley left me. The first person who can guess what Charley's secret was will win it as a prize." As the children gasped, the banker gave Miss McCabe a wink. "Bein' that Charley liked young people so, I think he'd approve, don't you?

"So what about it? Does anybody care to make a guess? Think about all the things I told you about Charley."

Bewildered, the students looked at each other and then back at Mr. Perkins.

"He wasn't secretly a bandit, was he?" Alex asked uncertainly. "Like Black Bart?"

"That's dumb, Alex," Jimmy said impatiently. "He doesn't sound anything like a bandit. Besides, he was a hero, right, Mr. Perkins?"

"I certainly think so," Mr. Perkins nodded. "And no, he wasn't any kind of bandit—although, considerin' the story of Black Bart, that isn't a bad guess."

"You said he was an orphan," Pablo said thoughtfully.

"Does the secret have to do with who his parents were? Did it turn out that he came from some famous family or something like that?"

Mr. Perkins shook his head. "That's an interesting notion, but so far as I know, Charley's fame was all his own. Any more guesses?"

Frowning in concentration, Margaret tried to think of some clue they were all forgetting. Suddenly she felt a poke in her back. "Psst," Peter whispered. "Have you got it, Smarty?" Without turning around, she gave a little shake of her head.

"Did you have a guess, Peter?" Miss McCabe asked.

"Um, no, ma'am," Peter mumbled.

"Anyone else? No? Then it seems we all give up," Miss McCabe said to Mr. Perkins.

"Well, don't feel too bad," said Mr. Perkins. "The fact is, Charley's secret was so amazin' that you could have knocked his friends and neighbors over with a feather when they heard the news. It came from the doctor or undertaker, I'm not such which, who was checkin' Charley's body and preparin' it for burial. It was then that Charley's secret was discovered at last." Pausing, the banker took a deep breath.

"Strange as it seems, old One-Eyed Charley, the famed Knight of the Road—and maybe the best and bravest whip California had ever seen—was . . ."

Margaret nearly jumped out of her seat. "A woman!" she blurted out.

"A woman?" Peter echoed in disbelief. "Don't be silly."

"That's *really* dumb, Sis," Alex put in.

Mr. Perkins's face broke into a wide grin. "I'm afraid she's right, boys. Charley Parkhurst—whom no man could beat at a man's trade—was indeed . . . a woman." As the boys gaped, he walked to Margaret's desk and laid a hand on her shoulder. "Looks like you win the prize, Miss. I guess you figured it out when I mentioned the body, is that right?"

Biting her lip, Margaret nodded. Tears were trickling

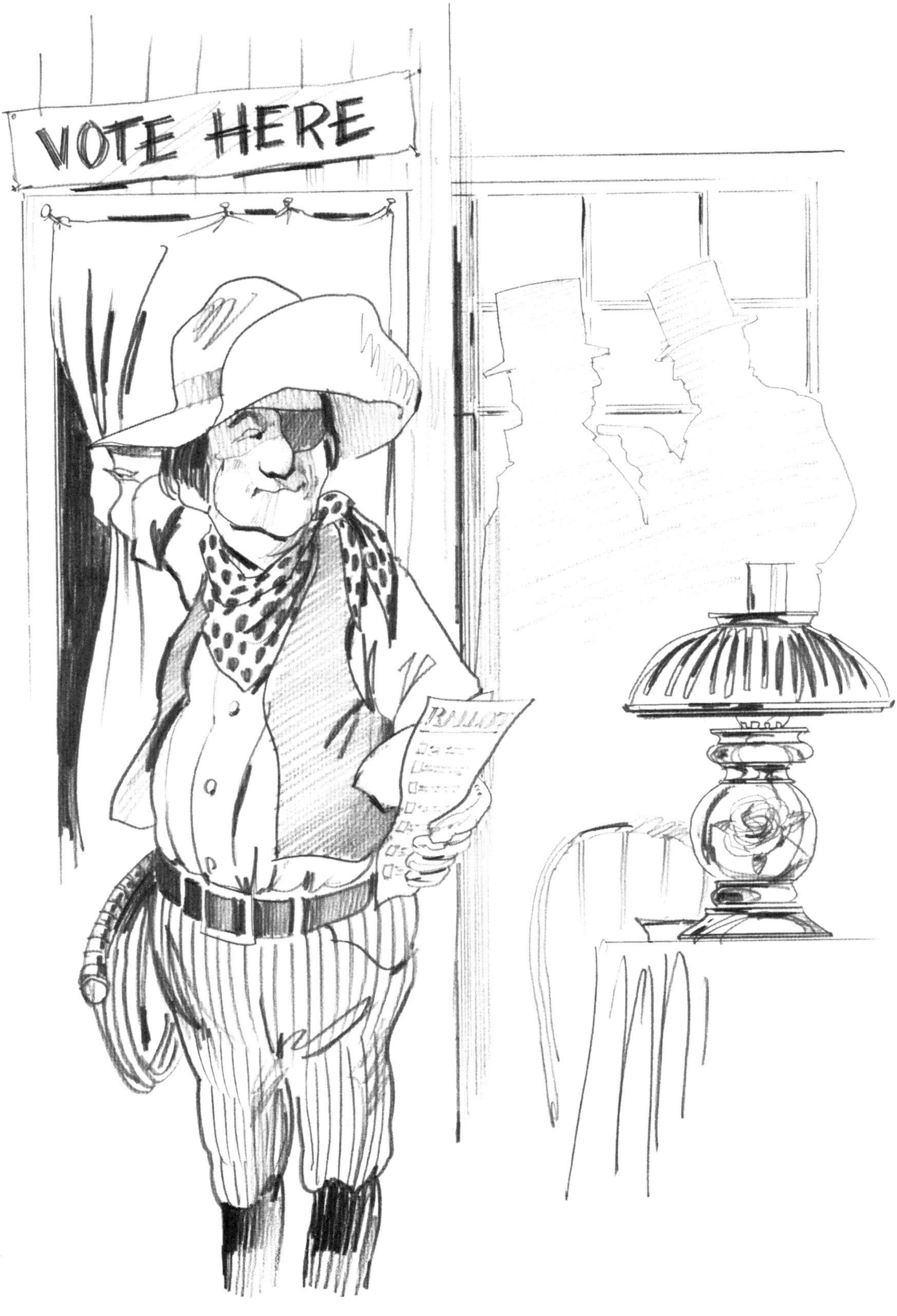
VOTE HERE
BALLOT

down her cheeks. "She must have been so lonesome," she whimpered.

Miss McCabe shook her head sadly. "What a pity," she murmured, "that she had to pretend to be a man to live the life she wanted to live."

Mr. Perkins nodded thoughtfully. "It's a pity, all right," he agreed. "But Charley's masquerade allowed her to make history—in more ways than one. For she was able to do something that no woman in the United States had the right to do until this very year, nineteen-hundred and twenty. Anybody know what that was?"

Miss McCabe caught her breath. "Why, of course!" she gasped. "You said that in 1868—"

"She voted for President of the United States!" Margaret finished.

"That's right, Miss," Mr. Perkins said, patting Margaret on the shoulder. He looked at each of the children in turn. "And that, my friends, makes Charley Parkhurst—or should I say, *Charlotte* Parkhurst—the first woman ever to vote in a United States presidential election!"

With a broad smile, Mr. Perkins reached for Margaret's hand. Gently he laid Charley's coin in her palm. "Voting is something you'll be able to do someday, Miss, when you're old enough. In the meantime, if anybody says you can't do something just because you're a girl, you show them this souvenir and tell 'em the tale of a genuine hero—One-Eyed Charley, the California Whip. That should teach 'em."

Blinking away her tears, Margaret gazed in wonder at the aged yellow coin that once had belonged to Charley Parkhurst.

"I will, Mr. Perkins," she promised. Closing her hand tightly around the heavy gold piece, she looked up into the banker's kindly face and smiled bravely.

"I will for sure."

# Author's Notes

Each book in the History and Happenings of California Series contains an Author's Notes section. These notes are an extension of the story and help to give an in-depth, factual look at the **people**, **places**, and **subjects** discussed in the text. Because of Charley Parkhurst's special place in California history, the Author's Notes are perhaps especially important to this work.

Although Margaret, Mr. Perkins, and the other characters associated with Manchester School are imaginary, the information Mr. Perkins conveys to the children in the story is based on historical research. In particular, it is important to note that **Charley Parkhurst** was a very real person—and that she was indeed the first woman who is known to have voted in a United States presidential election. Because of this distinction, and because of the theme of my retelling of her story, it was convenient to set this tale in the historic year of 1920—the year in which women's suffrage became a reality in national elections in the United States.

Thanks to the secret that was revealed only upon Charley's death, in subsequent years she became something of a celebrity. As often happens when celebrities are involved, over time a number of publications have printed stories about her life. However, as with other colorful characters of her day (such as gunslingers, gamblers, bandits, and miners, as well as other Knights of the Road), I discovered that a number of the accounts contained inaccurate—or exaggerated—information. Moreover, various sources describe the same events somewhat differently. Therefore, it is important to point out that even though incidents *similar* to those described by Mr. Perkins are believed to have taken place, many of the details are necessarily conjecture.

As difficult as it is to separate fact from fiction, history buffs who are familiar with Charley's story believe that her life was unique in the annals of California and the West—and indeed of the United States. Of course, a major question about Charley is why she chose to lead the life she did. Unfortunately, since she succeeded in maintaining her secret almost to the grave, we can only speculate about her reasons. Perhaps her saga began when she ran away from the orphanage. It may have been at this time that she cropped her hair short and first dressed as a boy, hoping to fool the stagecoach driver and enhance her chances of escape. Perhaps she figured it would be easier to make her way as a young lad, since in the first half of the nineteenth century a girl's place was thought to be in the home.

Whatever Charley's reasons, she was obviously successful in her masquerade. It seems appropriate that she eventually found her way to the Golden State, as colorful characters seemed to abound in California. Certainly a high point in the history of the thirty-first state—and an episode that brought colorful figures from far and wide—was the **Gold Rush**. This was the scene Charley found herself in when she ventured west to continue her stage-driving career.

The rush began, of course, with the discovery of gold by James W. Marshall on January 24, 1848, at a site on the American River, near the present-day town of Coloma. Californians of all descriptions soon converged on what became known as the **Gold Country,** including both the Mother Lode region (extending roughly from Mariposa, in present Mariposa County, northward to Placerville, in present El Dorado County) and the northern mines (extending north from Placerville to various communities along present Highway 49 and beyond). Although some women and children accompanied the miners, and southerners sometimes brought slaves to assist in the work, most of the gold seekers were young white males. As word of the discovery spread—particularly after President James Polk's official announcement in December 1848—people from around the globe, representing a diversity of ethnic groups, swelled the ranks of the **Forty-Niners.**

Mining camps with colorful names like those mentioned in our story sprang up virtually overnight. As the placer mines gave out, many of these disappeared or became ghost towns almost as quickly, but others became real towns. In addition to stone and brick buildings, some towns even boasted opera houses where entertainers like **Lola Montez** and **Lotta Crabtree** appeared. Those seeking the "Gold Country" town of **Manchester,** however, would do well to look elsewhere than the Sierra Nevada. Because the latter-day characters in my story are fictional, I made the community they lived in an imaginary one as well. However, there *was* a Manchester in a lesser-known Mother Lode, the Los Burros Mining District in the coastal Santa Lucia Mountains of south Monterey County. One of the legends behind the Manchester name is similar to the tale Mr. Perkins tells in the text.

As Mr. Perkins relates, stagecoach drivers were much admired by the Forty-Niners. Besides the names **"whips,"** **"Knights of the Road,"** and **"jehus"** (taken from a biblical term, and informally defined as a fast driver, a coachman), they were also known as "reinsmen," "hostlers," and "knights of the lash." Lord in his way and captain of his craft is the way Hubert Howe Bancroft, California's premier historian, described the stage drivers. Bancroft also indicated that the whips prided themselves on being experts in a profession they set above all others.

The termination point for many of the early California stage lines was **Sacramento.** By 1851, the year Charley is thought to have arrived in California, Sacramento was considered the hub of stagecoach travel in the Golden State. As an example of the numerous stages that constantly came and went, during a one-month period in 1853 a dozen different lines are estimated to have terminated there. The following year—with Sacramento becoming California's capital city—stagecoaching added color and excitement to the overall scene. It was also in 1854 that the famed **California Stage Company** (with which **James Birch** and **Frank**

**Stevens** were affiliated) established its headquarters in the capital city's popular **Orleans Hotel.**

The mainstay of the stage lines was the **Concord Coach,** which boasted shock-absorbing leather straps (thoroughbraces) that supported the body and guaranteed the comfort of passengers. The Concords were built by the Abbot-Downing Company of Concord, New Hampshire (thus the origin of their name). Considered the finest road vehicles of their day, they were built so sturdily that they were able to withstand the deep-rutted, rock-filled roads of the West. Despite their cost—plus the expense and difficulty of transporting them to California—they became familiar sights throughout much of the state.

Perched atop his Concord Coach, a California whip truly was king of the road. Many of the drivers gained considerable fame throughout the West. Among the jehus mentioned by Mr. Perkins, **Hank Monk** was probably the best known, thanks to the famous trip involving **Horace Greeley** and written about by noted author and lecturer Artemus Ward as well as by **Mark Twain.**

**John Reynolds,** the second whip mentioned in the text, was considered one of the state's top drivers. One of his most talked-about outings took place in 1868. During that run he drove an eight-horse team pulling a fully loaded coach (boasting nine people inside and six on top) from Wilmington to Los Angeles—a distance of more than twenty miles—in the record time of one hour and seventeen minutes!

Black driver **George Monroe** was also ranked among California's best. Tragically killed by a mule in 1886, Monroe was later given a unique honor when Monroe Meadows in Yosemite National Park was named after him.

The "old man" of California's whips was **Dave Berry,** whose claims to fame include the fantastic record of having ridden half a million miles on the box. **Jim Miller,** the last whip named by Mr. Perkins, drove stages in both the Gold Country and the coastal mountains. Still discussed are

"Uncle Jim's" colorful accounts of California's badmen, including the legendary **Black Bart.**

Bandits, of course, were a real fact of life for California's stage drivers. Of these, Black Bart is one of the most notorious—not only because of his success as a highwayman, but because of the astonishing revelation that the famed outlaw was in fact the well-known San Francisco society gentleman Charles E. Bolton. Born Charles E. Boles, the future "Black Bart" apparently took up highwaymanship when his legal attempts to find gold proved disappointing. One source indicates that Bart may have borrowed a page from **Sugarfoot,** the bandit Charley is reputed to have killed. According to this source, Bart wore large socks over his boots to disguise his footprints. At the scene of at least two of his early robberies, this colorful outlaw left short poems signed "Black Bart, the PO8."

Unfortunately, information about Sugarfoot seems to be sketchy at best. I should mention that among the conflicting accounts of his encounters with Charley, some sources suggest that Sugarfoot was not alone when he attacked Charley's stage and that he was killed with a rifle, or shotgun, rather than a pistol.

In contrast to the case of Sugarfoot, one does not have to look far to find information about the bandits **Joaquin Murrieta** and **Three-Fingered Jack.** Not only were they sidekicks while alive—and among the most feared of all Mother Lode marauders—but they were reputed to have met death together in a shootout with the California Rangers near the Fresno County community of Coalinga. The story does not end there, however, as to this day there is considerable doubt whether the man who died with Three-Fingered Jack in that Cantua Canyon shootout was, in fact, the notorious Joaquin Murrieta.

For those of you who have become fascinated by bandits, stagecoaches, and the fact that Charley Parkhurst was a woman, a further note may be of interest: The last stagecoach robbery in the United States was performed by a young woman! For more information about this female road agent, you may want to look into the life of Pearl Hart.

While guns were the tools of the trade for California's badmen, it was the **whip** that symbolized the stage driver. Many stories are told of the drivers' prowess with the whip. An added example demonstrating Charley's ability and reputation may be of interest at this point. If we can believe the source, with a mere flick of her whip she could snip the end off an envelope or cut a cigar from a man's lips—at a distance of fifteen paces!

The same source describes Charley as standing approximately five feet, seven inches tall, with broad shoulders and long, well-developed arms. She also reportedly had a sun-tanned, beardless face. Other sources add that she weighed around 175 pounds, one account stating that she was on the short and stocky side.

As to Charley's attire, several writers mention that she favored an extra-wide leather belt, perhaps (as has been hinted) to help disguise her figure. Because she wore gloves in both summer and winter, one writer wondered whether they were used to hide a pair of small, feminine hands. Charley's homemade, box-pleated shirts have also prompted speculation that they were designed to contribute to her disguise. Much of her other outer wear—including her broad Texas felt hat—matched the mountain finery of her fellow whips. And, like so many folks of her day, she was seldom seen without a chew of tobacco tucked in her cheek.

In her later years, Charley took on a decidedly unique appearance thanks to the patch she wore over one eye. Although a number of sources describe the incident that cost Charley her left eye as taking place in the **Redwood City** area when she was shoeing a horse, one source gives a different version of the accident. This account states that the problem arose when Charley stopped her team to soothe a horse that had been spooked by a rattlesnake. Unfortunately, the excited animal reportedly kicked Charley in the face as she tried to calm it down. As is so often the case with Charley's life, we are once again faced with conjecture. There is no doubt, however, that some such accident led to her acquiring the nickname One-Eyed Charley.

Because different sources depict similar situations in a variety of ways, a certain literary license is inevitable in re-creating the details of scenes from Charley's life, including some of those connected with the Tuolumne River adventure. I should also mention that the portion of the text that portrays Charley and other whips running over money in the road comes more from stories that have been passed on than from well-documented accounts. However, written accounts do describe the "show" the Knights of the Road put on when they came highballing into town. As to running over coins in the road, sources describing events in **Watsonville** tell of Charley's ability to run the front and rear wheels of her stage over money in the road while driving at a fast clip.

Speaking of Watsonville, the races that took place in and around the **Monterey Bay** area must indeed have been exciting to see! The finish line for several of these impromptu events was at an establishment known as Howe's Half Way House, which was located near the valley town of Salinas. Howe's was a popular gathering place that catered to locals as well as travelers. It was here that whiskey is said to have flowed freely while bets were made on which stage would reach the stop first. Often the coaches came from opposite directions (outbound from communities both north and south). Upon reaching Howe's in a cloud of dust, the whips and their passengers were greeted by a boisterous crowd of onlookers who raised their glasses in salute and cheered their arrival. Of interest to Charley fans is a comment from one source stating that entire cases of whiskey were bet on her bravery, daring, and skill. A second source adds that she was usually the first to arrive on the scene.

When Charley finally hung up her whip, she took to

operating a stage stop. The exact location of the stop is a matter of some dispute, with one account stating that she opened a "stage station" north of **Santa Cruz,** on the road from Santa Cruz to Los Gatos. It was in this general area that Charley reportedly purchased a ranch and gave it to a widow and her daughter so they wouldn't have to move. In this connection, I might mention that during Charley's days as a whip, she was considered the "king" of the San Jose to Santa Cruz run, which passed through the Los Gatos area. Moreover, when other jehus were unable to make the trip, she did "double duty" by driving both ways. This was quite a feat, as the run crossed the rugged **Santa Cruz Mountains.**

Most sources, however, place Charley's stage stop east of Santa Cruz, on the Santa Cruz to Watsonville run. The stop is described as both a halfway house and a way station, with mention being made of Charley's "furnishing refreshments for man and beast." Of course, facilities for changing horses were also available.

It is possible that the stage stop was also the site of the small ranch or farm Charley acquired after she gave up driving stages. In all probability, the land she lived on during the latter part of the 1860s was located somewhere between Santa Cruz and Watsonville, probably near the community of Soquel. While there Charley is said to have raised livestock as well as a limited number of crops, including hay, wheat, and apples. Her homemade hard cider is said to have been a favorite among the locals.

During this time Charley is also described in more than one account as having worked as a logger in nearby Santa Cruz Mountain lumber camps. She is said to have been skillful with an axe, and supposedly she earned more than the average lumberjack. Whether these reports are accurate is impossible to say.

Most accounts agree that it was sometime during the early to middle 1870s that Charley gave up farming and moved to the cabin near Watsonville where she spent the rest of her days. The cabin was evidently on property owned by the **Harmon** family. The Harmons were friends of Charley's and were among the people who watched over her during her fatal illness. One of them was the young **Harmon boy,** who is described as having been "nice" to Charley in her "declining years." As Mr. Perkins relates, Charley liked children and is reported to have left her savings to young Harmon.

Now that we know the aged whip's secret, we can guess why she did not go to a doctor when she was ill. However, several writers mention that Charley did visit a local "cancer man," who suggested placing a silver tube in her throat to help her breath. Charley refused, and according to one source treated her ailment with a "horse remedy" instead.

In a previous story I wrote about Charley, I indicated that she wasn't alone when she died. However, after continued research I find myself leaning the other way. With more than one hundred years having passed since Charley's death, I doubt that anyone will ever know for sure.

It was after she died, of course, that Charley's secret became known. Only later was her fame enhanced by the discovery that on November 3, 1868, she voted for President. This claim to fame is memorialized today on Charley's gravestone in the Pioneer Cemetery in Watsonville. Erected by the Pajaro Valley Historical Association, the gravestone credits this "noted whip of the Gold Rush days" with being "the first woman to vote in the United States."

It was not until August 26, 1920, that women officially gained the right to vote in federal elections with the ratification of the 19th Amendment to the U.S. Constitution. To put Charley's voting into better perspective, I might note that she cast her vote a year earlier than a woman in the United States could openly vote even in a state or territorial election. Wyoming, with its strong tradition of pioneer women, scored a historic "first" by granting women the vote in 1869, while it was still a territory. It was in the same year of 1869 that Susan B. Anthony and **Elizabeth Cady Stanton** organized the National Woman Suffrage Association. (Incidentally, an important figure in the suffrage movement—sometimes allied with Elizabeth Cady Stanton and sometimes disagreeing with her—was none other than publisher Horace Greeley, who "enjoyed" that famous ride in Hank Monk's stage.) In California, agitation for women's suffrage was making headline news by 1870, but the long campaign did not achieve success until the state constitution was amended in 1911.

Charley Parkhurst had already proved that a woman could succeed in what was thought to be strictly a man's profession. Was she making a sly statement on behalf of her sex in 1868? Did she think that one day her secret would be discovered? We will probably never know.

Early on the morning of December 29, 1979, the one-hundredth anniversary of Charley Parkhurst's death, my wife and I visited Watsonville's Pioneer Cemetery. While we were there we placed a pine bough, tied with a red ribbon, on Charley's grave. We were alone in the cemetery at the time, and as we stood by Charley's side we thought about her remarkable life—and how little anyone really knows about her. As I complete these notes, I can't help but think that Charley might be chuckling over the fact that some of the pieces of her puzzle will probably never be found. I have a suspicion that that is exactly the way she would like it to be.

# *About the Author*

Randall A. Reinstedt was born and raised on California's beautiful and historic Monterey Peninsula. After traveling widely throughout the world, he spent fifteen years teaching elementary school students, with special emphasis on California and local history. Today he continues to share his love of California's beauty and lore with young and old alike through his immensely popular publications. Among his many books is **More Than Memories: History & Happenings of the Monterey Peninsula**, an acclaimed history text for fourth-graders that is used in schools throughout the Monterey area.

Randy lives with his wife, Debbie, and son, Erick, in a house overlooking the Pacific Ocean. In addition to his writing projects, he is in great demand as a lecturer on regional history to school and adult groups, and he frequently gives workshops for teachers on making history come alive in the classroom.

# *About the Illustrator*

A native Californian, Ed Greco has spent most of his professional career as a graphic designer and illustrator. Born and raised in the Santa Clara Valley, Ed grew up studying and illustrating northern California, its environment, and its history.

## Randall A. Reinstedt's
# *History & Happenings of California Series*

Through colorful tales drawn from the rich store of California lore, this series introduces young readers to the historical heritage of California and the West. "Author's Notes" at the end of each volume provide information about the people, places, and events encountered in the text. Whether read for enjoyment or for learning, the books in this series bring the drama and adventure of yesterday to the young people of today.

Currently available:

**One-Eyed Charley, the California Whip**
ISBN 0-933818-23-8

**Otters, Octopuses, and Odd Creatures of the Deep**
ISBN 0-933818-21-1

**Stagecoach Santa**
ISBN 0-933818-20-3

**The Strange Case of the Ghosts of the Robert Louis Stevenson House**
ISBN 0-933818-22-X

*California history and lore are also featured in Randy Reinstedt's books for adults and older children. For information about these titles, please write Ghost Town Publications, P.O. Drawer 5998, Carmel, California 93921*